Road Atlas of SOUTH AFRICA

NEW HOLLAND

New Holland (Publishers) Ltd
London • Cape Town • Sydney • Singapore

First edition   1994
Second impression   1995
Third impression   1996
Fourth impression   1997
Second edition   1997

24 Nutford Place
London W1H 6DQ
United Kingdom

80 McKenzie Street
Cape Town 8001
South Africa

3/2 Aquatic Drive
Frenchs Forest, NSW 2086
Australia

ISBN 1 85368 847 9

Publishing Manager: Mariëlle Renssen
Text: Peter Joyce, Claudia Dos Santos
Editor: Claudia Dos Santos
Design and DTP: Lyndall du Toit,
Claudia Dos Santos
Project Cartographer: John Loubser
Compiler/Verifier: Elaine Fick

Reproduction by cmyk pre-press, Cape Town
Printed and bound by National Book Printers
P O Box 120, Parow 7500, Republic of South Africa

Cover: *The noble and graceful kudu is one of South Africa's best-loved antelopes.*
Title page: *The picturesque Wilderness coastline, part of the well-known Garden Route, is a popular destination for visitors.*

Photographic Credits

Photo Access/Walter Knirr, page 10; **Herman Potgieter**, page 33; **SIL/Shaen Adey**, pages 49, 59; **SIL/CLB**, page 24; **SIL/Roger de la Harpe**, pages 30, 67; **SIL/Gerhard Dreyer**, title page, page 40; **SIL/Walter Knirr**, pages 16, 18, 54, 70 (bottom), 72, 80; **SIL/Peter Pickford**, page 74; **SIL/Erhardt Thiel**, pages 46, 48, 53; **SIL/Hein von Hörsten**, pages 35, 39, 62; **SIL/Lanz von Hörsten**, front cover, pages 20, 42, 45, 78; **SIL/Keith Young**, pages 26, 28, 57, 61, 70 (top); [SIL: Struik Image Library; CLB: Colour Library]

Emergency Telephone Numbers
Notrufnummern
Appels d'Urgence

Police Polizeirevier Poste de police	**10111**
Telephone enquiries Telefon Auskunft Information téléphonique	**1023**
Ambulance Krankenwagen Ambulances	**10177**

This brightly coloured South African flag was first raised at midnight on 26 April 1994. For most South Africans it is a symbol of hope, uniting the nation in their effort to reconciliate and become a truly democratic society.

CONTENTS

KEY TOURIST AREAS

MAIN MAP SECTION

INDEX

For ease of use, the **INDEX** has been divided into two sections:

- the first focuses on the **KEY TOURIST AREA MAPS** and related text and photographs.

- the second deals with the **MAIN MAP SECTION** only, facilitating the easy location of cities, towns and villages.

NATIONAL ROUTE PLANNER

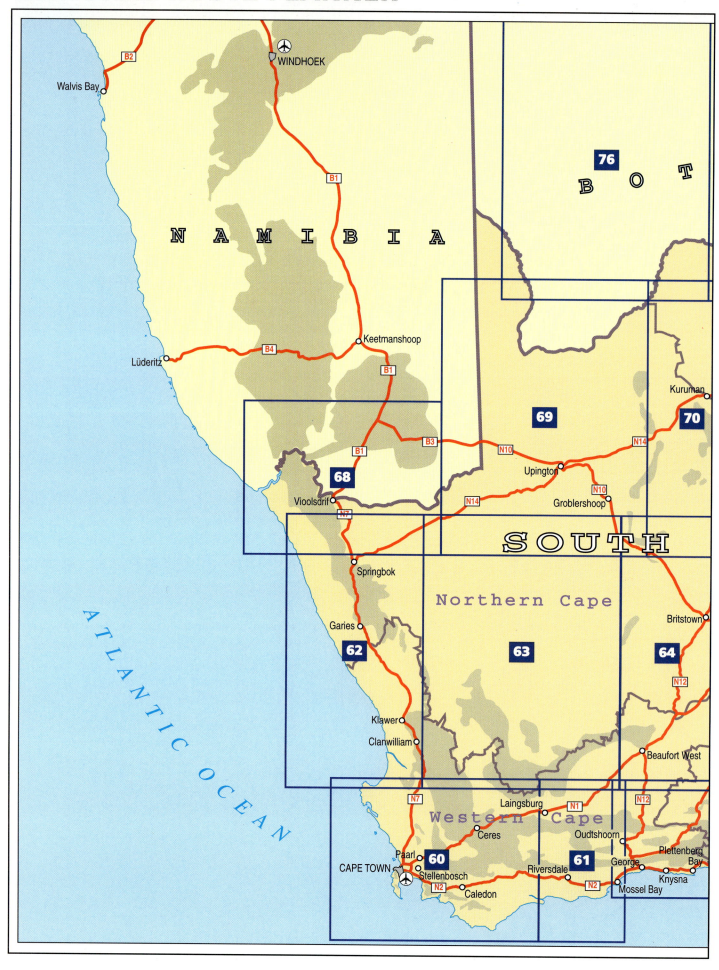

KEY TOURIST AREAS

ZIMBABWE

MOZAMBIQUE

Messina

21

Northern Province

PIETERSBURG

Phalaborwa

Potgietersrus

11 Warm Baths

22 N1

KRUGER NATIONAL PARK

19

Rustenburg

17 PRETORIA

N4

N4 Nelspruit

23

North West **14-15** JOHANNESBURG

Middelburg

MAPUTO

N12

13

N17

Heidelberg

Mpumalanga

Mbabane

SWAZILAND

N12

N14

55

N12

Klerksdorp

N3

Ermelo

N11

32

Volksrust

25

Newcastle

57 KIMBERLEY

N1

Bethlehem

Harrismith

KwaZulu-Natal

N5

Winburg

31

St Lucia

56

BLOEMFONTEIN

Ladysmith

Richards Bay

N8

AFRICA

MASERU

THE NATAL DRAKENSBERG PARK

N2

N12

LESOTHO

29 PIETERMARITZBURG

N3

27

N12

N1

Aliwal North

DURBAN **29**

N10

N2

Hanover

N6

Eastern Cape

Port Shepstone

N1

Middelburg

UMTATA

Port Edward

Queenstown

N2

Cradock

33

N10

N9

34

35

Grahamstown

N2

EAST LONDON **37**

I N D I A N   O C E A N

N2

PORT ELIZABETH **36**

N

0 _____ 200 km	**33** Page numbers	National route ——— National route number N12
0 _____ 100 miles		International boundary ——— City, town & village
		Provincial boundary ——— International airport ✈

National route — National route number N12
International boundary — City, town & village
Provincial boundary — International airport

DISTANCE CHART

APPROXIMATE DISTANCES IN KILOMETRES	BLOEMFONTEIN	CAPE TOWN	DURBAN	EAST LONDON	GABORONE	GRAHAMSTOWN	JOHANNESBURG	KIMBERLEY	MAPUTO	MASERU	MBABANE	PORT ELIZABETH	PRETORIA	WELKOM	WINDHOEK
BEAUFORT WEST	547	457	1178	605	1042	492	942	504	1349	609	1129	501	1000	697	1629
BLOEMFONTEIN		1004	634	584	622	601	398	177	897	157	677	677	456	153	1593
BRITSTOWN	398	710	1032	609	791	496	725	253	1289	555	1075	572	783	551	1378
CAPE TOWN	1004		1753	1099	1501	899	1402	962	1900	1160	1680	769	1460	1156	1500
COLESBERG	228	778	860	488	848	375	624	292	1123	383	903	451	682	379	1573
DE AAR	346	762	980	557	843	444	744	305	1243	503	1023	520	802	499	1430
DURBAN	634	1753		674	979	854	578	811	625	590	562	984	636	564	2227
EAST LONDON	584	1079	674		1206	180	982	780	1301	630	1238	310	1040	737	1987
GABORONE	622	1501	979	1206		1223	358	538	957	702	719	1299	350	479	1735
GEORGE	773	438	1319	645	1361	465	1171	762	1670	913	1450	335	1229	926	1887
GRAAFF-REINET	424	787	942	395	1012	282	822	490	1321	599	1101	291	880	577	1697
GRAHAMSTOWN	601	899	854	172	1223		999	667	1478	692	1418	138	1057	754	1856
HARRISMITH	328	1331	306	822	673	929	274	505	649	284	468	1068	332	258	1921
JOHANNESBURG	398	1402	578	982	358	899		472	599	438	361	1075	58	258	1801
KEETMANSHOOP	1088	995	1722	1482	1230	1351	1296	911	1869	1245	1651	1445	1351	1205	505
KIMBERLEY	177	962	811	780	538	667	472		1071	334	833	743	530	294	1416
KLERKSDORP	288	1271	645	872	334	889	164	308	763	368	525	1009	222	145	1693
KROONSTAD	211	1214	537	795	442	812	187	339	742	247	522	888	245	71	1724
LADYSMITH	410	1413	236	752	755	932	356	587	567	366	386	1062	414	340	2008
MAFIKENG	464	1343	821	1048	158	1065	287	380	886	544	648	1141	294	321	1577
MAPUTO	897	1900	625	1301	957	1478	599	1071		853	223	1609	583	813	2400
MASERU	157	1160	590	630	702	692	438	334	853		633	822	488	249	1750
MBABANE	677	1680	562	1238	719	1418	361	833	223	633		1548	372	451	2162
MESSINA	928	1932	1118	1512	696	1529	530	1002	725	960	808	1605	476	788	2331
NELSPRUIT	757	1762	707	1226	672	1358	355	827	244	713	173	1434	322	639	2156
OUDTSHOORN	743	506	1294	704	1241	532	1141	703	1705	959	1417	394	1199	896	1950
PIETERMARITZBURG	555	1674	79	595	900	775	499	732	706	511	640	905	557	485	2148
PIETERSBURG	717	1721	897	1301	485	1318	319	791	605	749	515	1394	267	577	2120
PORT ELIZABETH	677	769	984	310	1299	130	1075	743	1609	822	1548		1133	830	1950
PRETORIA	456	1460	636	1040	350	1057	58	530	583	488	372	1133		316	1859
QUEENSTOWN	377	1069	676	207	999	269	775	554	1302	423	1240	399	833	525	1829
UMTATA	570	1314	439	235	1192	415	869	747	1064	616	1003	545	928	718	2066
UPINGTON	588	894	1222	982	730	851	796	411	1395	745	1157	945	854	669	1005
WELKOM	153	1156	564	737	479	754	258	294	813	249	451	830	316		1679
WINDHOEK	1593	1500	2227	1987	1735	1856	1801	1416	2400	1750	2162	1950	1859	1679	

DISTANCE IN KM FROM CAPE TOWN	
Bloemfontein	1004
Durban	1753
Johannesburg	1402
Kimberley	962
Port Elizabeth	769

Distance Charts

In order to calculate the distance between two of the country's major centres, locate the name of the first town or city on the vertical or horizontal column on the chart (see left), then locate the name of the other on the second column and read off the number where the vertical and horizontal lines intersect.

CAPE TOWN	J	F	M	A	M	J	J	A	S	O	N	D
AV. TEMP. °C	21	21	20	17	15	13	12	13	14	16	18	20
AV. TEMP. °F	70	70	68	63	59	55	54	55	57	61	64	68
DAILY SUN hrs	11	10	9	7	6	6	6	7	8	9	10	11
RAINFALL mm	14	17	19	39	74	92	70	75	39	37	15	17
RAINFALL in	0.6	0.7	0.7	2	3	4	3	3	2	1.5	0.6	0.7
SEA TEMP. °C	15	14	13	13	12	12	12	13	13	14	14	14
SEA TEMP. °F	59	57	55	55	54	54	54	55	55	57	57	57

Climate Charts

Above is an example of a Climate Chart. These occur throughout the atlas, and give the average temperatures and rainfall for the relevant region or city.

Toll Road Chart

Various South African provinces are served by time-saving toll roads. The chart below identifies the names of these toll roads, the locations of the toll plazas, points between which the toll roads stretch and grid references for locating these roads on the maps in this book.

TOLL ROADS

Strip Routes

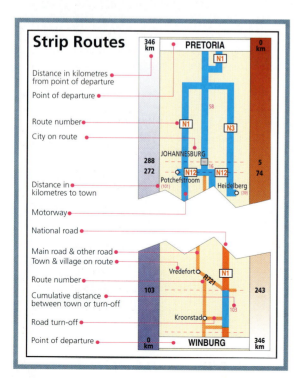

- Distance in kilometres from point of departure
- Point of departure
- Route number
- City on route
- Distance in kilometres to town
- Motorway
- National road
- Main road & other road
- Town & village on route
- Route number
- Cumulative distance between town or turn-off
- Road turn-off
- Point of departure

TOLL ROADS Ⓣ				
ROUTE	PROVINCE	NAME	TOLL PLAZA	LOCATION
N1	Western Cape	HUGUENOT TUNNEL	HUGUENOT	DU TOITS KLOOF
N1	Free State	KROONVAAL	VAAL	UNCLE CHARLIES–KROONSTAD
N1	Gauteng		GRASMERE	JHB–VANDERBIJLPARK
N1	Northern Province	KRANSKOP	KRANSKOP	WARMBATHS–MIDDELFONTEIN
N2	Western Cape	TSITSIKAMMA	TSITSIKAMMA	THE CRAGS & STORMS RIVER
N2	KwaZulu-Natal	SOUTH COAST	ORIBI	SOUTHBROOM–MARBURG
N2	KwaZulu-Natal		IZOTSHA	SOUTHBROOM–MARBURG
N2	KwaZulu-Natal	NORTH COAST	TONGAAT	UMDLOTI–BALLITO
N2	KwaZulu-Natal		UMVOTI	SHAKASKRAAL / STANGER
N2	KwaZulu-Natal		MTUNZINI	MTUNZINI / FELIXTON
N3	Free State	HIGHVELD	WILGE	VILLIERS–WARDEN
N3	KwaZulu-Natal	MIDLANDS	TUGELA	KEEVERSFONTEIN–FRERE
N3	KwaZulu-Natal		MOOI RIVER	FRERE–CEDARA
N3	KwaZulu-Natal	MARIANNHILL	MARIANNHILL	ASSAGAY–PINETOWN
N4	Gauteng	MAGALIES	QUAGGA	PRETORIA–ATTERIDGEVILLE
N4	Gauteng		PELINDABA	ATTERIDGEVILLE–PELINDABA
N17	Gauteng	WITWATERSRAND	DALPARK	SPRINGS–DALPARK
N17	Gauteng		DENNE ROAD	SPRINGS–DALPARK
N17	Gauteng		GOSFORTH	DALPARK–RAND AIRPORT

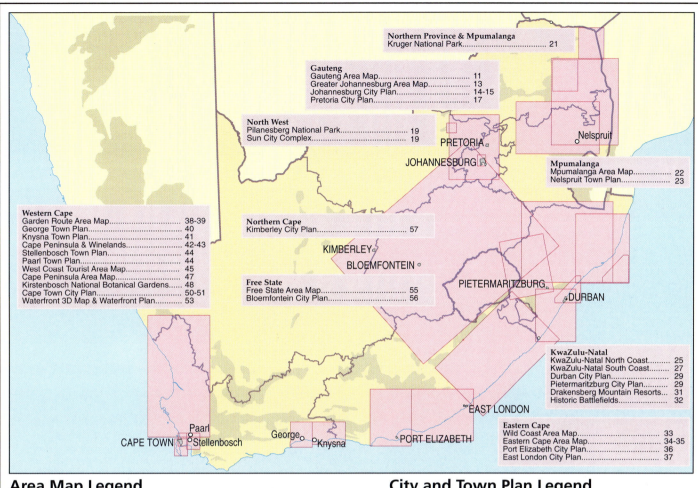

Area Map Legend

National road / Nationalstraße / Route nationale	
Motorway / Autobahn / Autoroute	
Principal road / Regionalstraße / Route de liaison régionale	
Main road / Hauptstraße / Route principale	Tarred — Untarred
Minor road / Nebenstraße / Route secondaire	Tarred — Untarred
Route numbers / Routenummern / Numéros de routes	N4 R28 R518
Distances in kilometres / Entfernungen in Kilometern / Distance en kilomètres	19 / 15
Scenic route / Malerische Landschaft / Route panoramique	
Mountain pass / Bergpass / Col	Du Toits
Motorway & interchange / Autobahn mit Kreuzungen / Autoroute avec échangeur	
Railway / Eisenbahn / Chemin de fer	
International boundary / Internationale Grenze / Frontière internationale	
Provincial boundary / Provinz Grenze / Frontière provinciale	
Game & nature reserve / Wild- und Naturschutzgebiet / Réserve naturelle	Inyati N.R.
Battle site / Ehemaliges Schlachtfeld / Lieu de bataille historique	Ulundi
Mountain range / Gebirge / Chaîne de montagnes	LEBOMBO
Border post / Grenzübergang / Poste de contrôle	Lebombo
Provincial name / Provinz / Nom du département	Western Cape
Airport / Flughafen / Aéroport	INT. Other
Place of interest / Sehenswürdigkeit / Endroit à voir	Baobab Tree
Railway station (selected) / Bahnhöfe (Auswahl) / Gare	
Area name / Gebiet / Nom de la région	Ciskei
Toll road / Gebührenpfl. Straße / Route à péage	T
Peak in metres / Höhe in Metern / Sommet (en mètres)	Table Mtn. 1140m
Water feature / Gewässer / Hydrographie	River / Dam / Swamp
Safe bathing beach / Geschützter Badestrand / Baignade autorisée	
Major petrol stop / Große Tankstelle / Station-service	
Hotel (selected) / Hotel (Auswahl) / Hôtel	H
Camp / Ferienlager / Camp	

City and Town Plan Legend

Motorway and slip road / Autobahn mit Ausfahrt / Autoroute et jonction	
Main road and mall / Haupt- und Einkaufsstraßen / Route principale et Mall	MALL
Road / Straße / Route	
Railway / Eisenbahn / Chemin de fer	
Park and sports field / Park und Sportplatz / Parc et terrain de sports	
Route numbers / Routenummern / Numéros de routes	24 4 27
Hospital / Krankenhaus / Hôpital	
Caravan park / Wohnwagenpark / Camping pour caravanes	
Hotel / Hotel / Hôtel	MANOR H
Bus terminus / Endstation / Terminus d'autobus	
Building of interest / Wichtiges Bauwerk / Monument à voir	
Place of interest / Sehenswürdigkeit / Endroit à voir	Castle
Place of worship / Gotteshaus / Lieu du culte	
Police station / Polizeirevier / Poste de police	
Parking area / Parkplatz / Parking	P
Post office / Postamt / Bureau de poste	
Information centre / Auskunftsbüro / Centre d'information	i
Library / Bibliothek / Bibliothèque	
Built-up area / Wohngebiet / Agglomération	
One-way street / Einbahnstraße / Rue à sens-unique	→
Golf course / Golfplatz / Terrain de golf	
Major petrol stop / Große Tankstelle / Station-service	

City / Großstadt / Grande ville	Small town / Kleinstadt / Grand village
Major town / Bedeutende Stadt / Ville	Large village / Größere Ortschaft / Village
Town / Stadt / Ville secondaire	Village / Dorf / Petit village

GAUTENG

Johannesburg, bustling financial capital of Gauteng and South Africa's largest metropolis, and stately Pretoria, the country's administrative capital, are located 56km (35 miles) apart on the highest part of the interior plateau known as the Highveld. South of Johannesburg sprawls the urban conglomerate of Soweto, as well as a concentration of important industrial towns like Germiston, Vereeniging and Vanderbijlpark, while to the north lie Johannesburg's affluent garden suburbs. All these come together to form what is known as Gauteng – South Africa's pulsating economic heartland.

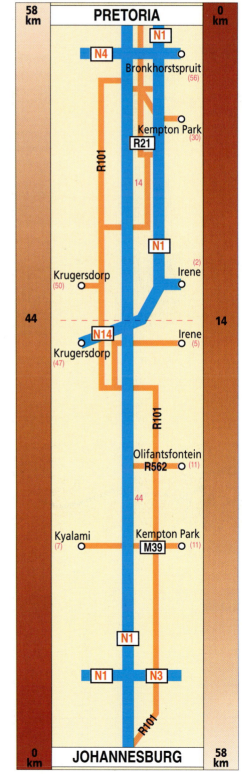

MAIN ATTRACTIONS

Johannesburg: South Africa's commercial and financial capital, a modern city dominated by concrete-and-glass giants.
Pretoria: the lovely 'Jacaranda City' offering a wealth of historic buildings; in October its avenues are strewn with lilac blossoms.
Sterkfontein Caves: northwest of Krugersdorp; source of artefacts from the dawn of humankind.

Hartbeespoort Dam: large body of water, picturesquely situated at the foothills of the Magaliesberg mountain range; popular with many anglers, campers and watersports enthusiasts.
Carousel Entertainment World and **Morula Sun:** dine in style, watch an entertaining show, or gamble the night away at one of these chic casino resorts.

DISTANCE IN KM FROM JOHANNESBURG	
Bloemfontein	398
Cape Town	1402
Durban	578
Nelspruit	355
Port Elizabeth	1075

USEFUL CONTACTS

Police, tel: 1-0111 (national number).
Ambulance, tel: 1-0177 (national number).
Johannesburg General Hospital, tel: (011) 488-4911, fax: 643-1612.
Johannesburg Metropolitan Tourism Association, tel: (011) 336-4961, fax: 336-4965; tourist information.
Computicket, tel: (011) 445-8445; for booking of theatre and cinema shows.
First National Bank, tel: (011) 371-1212; lost or stolen credit cards.
AA of South Africa, tel: (011) 799-1000.
SATOUR, Pretoria, tel: (012) 347-0600.

TRAVEL TIPS

A network of well-signposted roads and highways links the centres in this region. Speed limits apply to usual urban zones like schools and hospitals. As in crowded city areas worldwide, crime presents a growing problem. Common sense, however, goes a long way towards preventing potentially unpleasant situations. Below follow some safety guidelines:
• Plan your itinerary before setting out.
• Don't leave your vehicle if it is bumped from behind, but rather proceed to a populated and well-lit area.
• Never park in poorly lit areas.
• Don't walk around alone after dusk.
• Leave your personal belongings and valuables safely stored in the hotel when you venture out.

Below: The Randburg Waterfront, capturing the spirited ambience of a Mediterranean marina, has become a popular haunt for young and old alike.

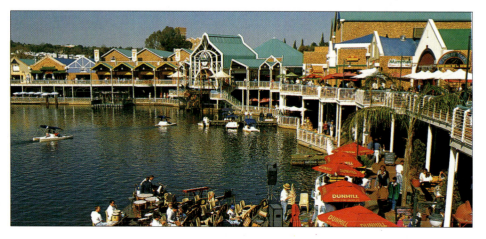

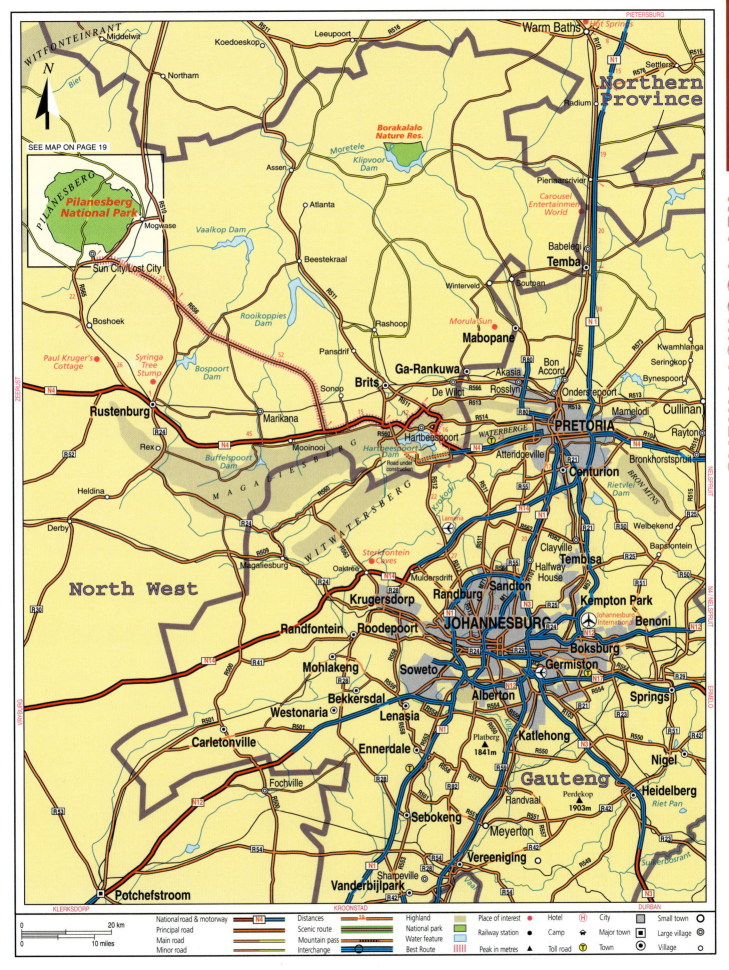

KEY TOURIST AREAS

GREATER JOHANNESBURG

The huge, yellow mine dumps and rusting headgear of the abandoned gold mines to the south of modern Johannesburg are evocative reminders of the days when the city was essentially a diggers' camp – a visit to Gold Reef City lets you relive the exciting gold-rush past. To the north, wealthy garden suburbs like Sandton and Randburg offer upmarket shopping centres, fashionable boutiques, souvenir shops, an impressive range of cosmopolitan and ethnic restaurants, and numerous entertainment venues. Informal art and craft markets are regularly held in the many parks, and there are no less than 11 challenging golf courses.

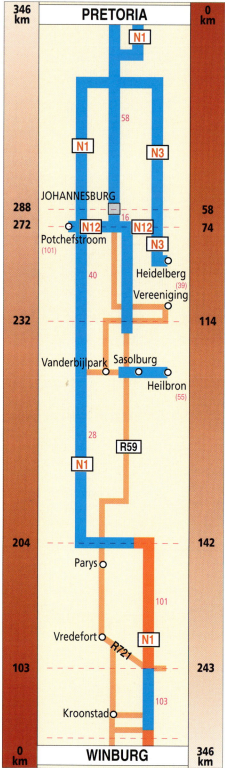

MAIN ATTRACTIONS

Gold Reef City: experience Johannesburg during the gold rush days. Descend deep into a mine, see traditional and 'gumboot' dances, visit the interesting museums and the fairground.

Randburg Waterfront: attractive complex with live entertainment, restaurants, shops and pubs.

MuseumAfrica: next to the Market Theatre; fascinating displays and artefacts illustrate South Africa's turbulent history from prehistory to the present.

Flea markets: the Johannesburg (at the Market Theatre) and Bruma Lake flea markets offer most anything, every Saturday.

Soweto: interesting tours with reputable operators give an insight into the birthplace of the country's freedom movement.

Traditional Herbalist Shop: at 14 Diagonal Street; marvel at the skins, bones, roots and herbs used by tribal doctors.

Events and Festivals

Lexington PGA Golf Tournament: International and Southern African golfing greats meet in **January** to fight it out for this prestigious title.

Rand Show: in **April** the National Exhibition Centre (southwest of Johannesburg) hosts the biggest consumer show in Africa, featuring local and international products.

Johannesburg Pops Festival: in **April** traditional and contemporary musicians, choirs and soloists get together for the most vibrant 3-day outdoor concert in southern Africa.

International Eisteddfod of South Africa: during **September/October** the city of Roodepoort hums with acitivity as musicians and dancers from around the world compete for honours in this cultural event.

Guinness Jazz Festival: in **September/October**; jazz extravaganza featuring exciting local and international talent.

JHB	J	F	M	A	M	J	J	A	S	O	N	D
AV. TEMP. °C	20	20	18	16	13	10	10	13	16	18	18	19
AV. TEMP. °F	68	68	64	61	55	50	50	55	61	64	64	66
DAILY SUN hrs	8	8	8	8	9	9	9	10	9	9	8	8
RAINFALL mm	131	95	81	55	19	7	6	6	26	72	114	106
RAINFALL in	5.5	4	3.5	2.5	0.7	0.3	0.2	0.2	1	3	4.5	4.5

ACCOMMODATION

Carlton Hotel ★★★★★, corner of Main and Kruis streets, tel: (011) 331-8911, fax: 331-3555; convenient, central location.

Holiday Inn Garden Court ★★★★, tel: (011) 336-7011, fax: 336-0515; in the city centre.

Sandton Sun and Towers Intercontinental ★★★★★, Sandton City, tel: (011) 780-5000, fax: 780-5002; luxurious accommodation.

Gold Reef Protea Hotel ★★★★, tel: (011) 496-1626, fax: 496-1636; Victorian charm, located right in the theme park.

City Lodge Morningside ★★★, tel: (011) 884-9500, fax: 884-9440; 30 minutes from the airport in lovely Sandton.

Holiday Inn Garden Court Milpark ★★★, Auckland Park, tel: (011) 726-5100, fax: 726-8615; some 6km (4½ miles) from the city centre.

Karos Johannesburger ★★★, tel: (011) 725-3753, fax: 725-6309; located in the heart of town.

Airport Formula One, tel: (011) 392-1453, fax: 974-3845; budget accommodation close to the International Airport.

City Lodge Airport, tel: 392-1750, fax: 392-2644; only 5 minutes from the airport.

Bed and Breakfast (central booking office), tel: (011) 482-2206, fax: 726-6915; assists travellers with finding accommodation.

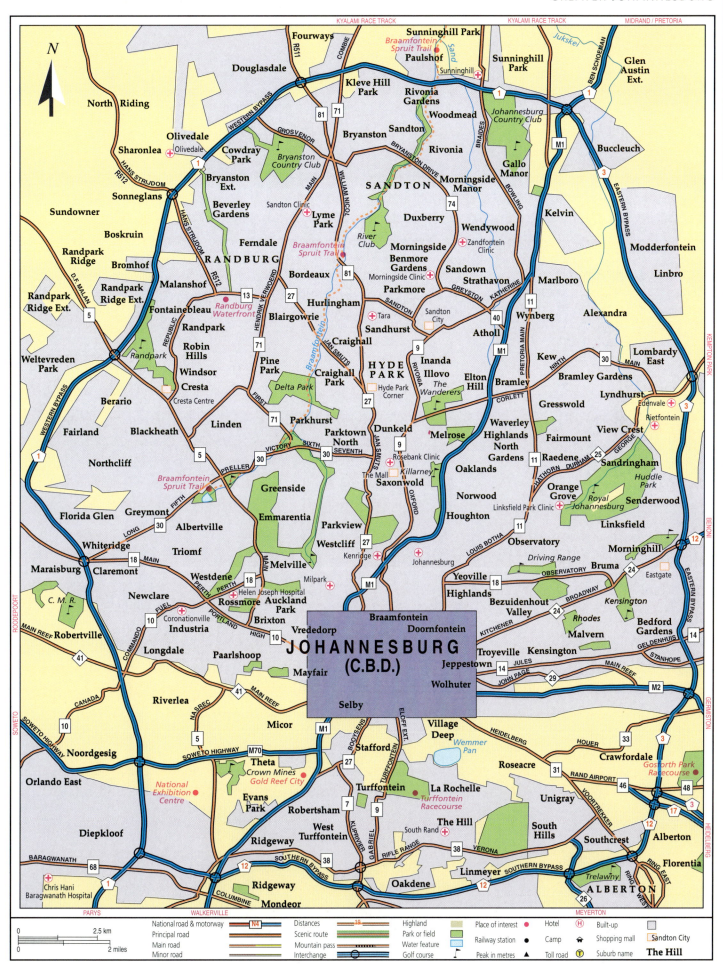

KEY TOURIST AREAS

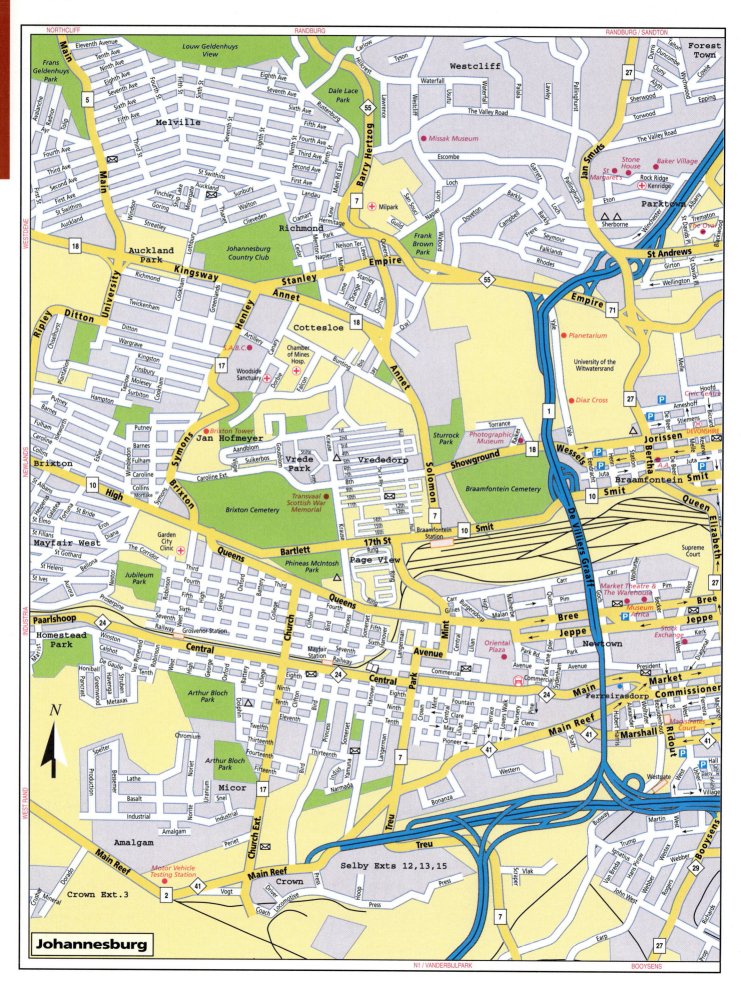

Johannesburg

14

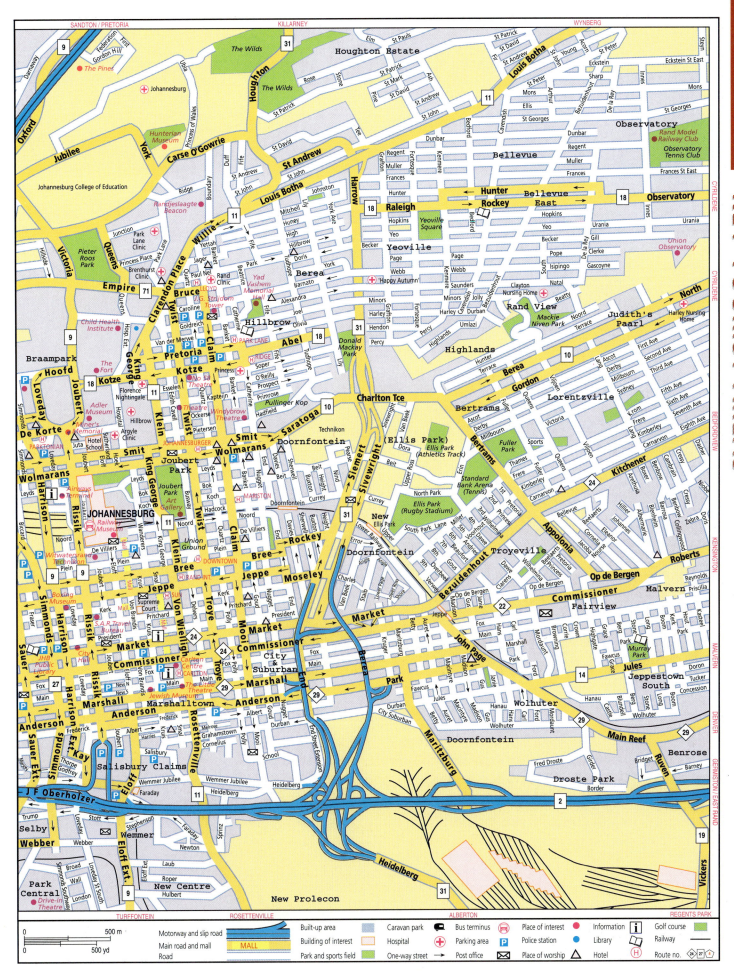

PRETORIA

*H*andsome Pretoria is noted for its stately, historic homes, the impressive Union Buildings (administrative seat of the South African government), its parks and gardens with their splendid wealth of indigenous flora, and for its tall jacaranda trees that transform the streets into a blaze of lilac each October/November, earning Pretoria its nickname. The city is the administrative capital of the country, as well as a centre of research and learning. Within its limits lie the Pretoria University; gigantic Unisa, the world's largest correspondence university; and Onderstepoort, an internationally renowned veterinary research institute.

MAIN ATTRACTIONS

Union Buildings: magnificent edifice designed by Sir Herbert Baker, on landscaped, terraced grounds that look out over the city from Meintjieskop.
Church Square: historic town square framed by beautiful old buildings such as the old Raadsaal (parliament), Palace of Justice and SA Reserve Bank.
Voortrekker Monument: construction on Monument Hill, 6km (4 miles) from the city, commemorating the Great Trek of the 1830 pioneers.
National Zoological Gardens: one of the world's largest; over 3500 exotic and indigenous species.
Transvaal Museum of Natural History: many extensive displays, including the impressive 'Life's Genesis' and the interesting Austin Roberts Bird Hall.
State Theatre: on completion in 1981, this imposing cultural complex, comprising five theatres and a public square, was the largest of its kind in the southern hemisphere.

Above: *Summer time in Pretoria is heralded by a glory of lilac blossoms as the many jacaranda trees begin to flower, covering city streets and walks with a fragrant, pastel-coloured carpet.*

PRETORIA	J	F	M	A	M	J	J	A	S	O	N	D
AV. TEMP. °C	23	22	21	18	15	11	12	14	18	20	21	22
AV. TEMP. °F	73	72	70	64	59	52	54	57	64	68	70	73
DAILY SUN hrs	9	8	8	8	9	9	9	10	10	9	9	9
RAINFALL mm	152	76	80	57	14	3	3	6	21	67	101	105
RAINFALL in	6	3	3.5	2.5	0.6	0.1	0.1	0.2	0.8	3	4	4.5

ACCOMMODATION

Centurion Lake Hotel ★★★★, 1001 Lenchen Avenue North, Centurion, tel: (012) 663-1825, fax: 663-2760.
Holiday Inn Crowne Plaza ★★★★, crn. Beatrix and Church streets, Arcadia, tel: (012) 341-1571, fax: 44-7534; centrally located.
Arcadia Hotel ★★★, tel: (012) 326-9311, fax: 326-1067; beautifully situated right at the foot of the impressive Union Buildings.

Bentley's Country Lodge ★★★, cnr. Main Street and Brits Road, Akasia, tel: (012) 542-1751, fax: 542-3487.
The Farm Inn ★★★, Lynwood Road, The Willows, tel: (012) 809-0266, fax: 809-0146; close to the city.
Madeleine Hotel, 562 Pretorius Street, tel: (012) 44-4281, fax: 341-7000; friendly establishment.
Panorama Inn, 706 Arcadia Street, tel: (012) 344-3010, fax: 343-8601.

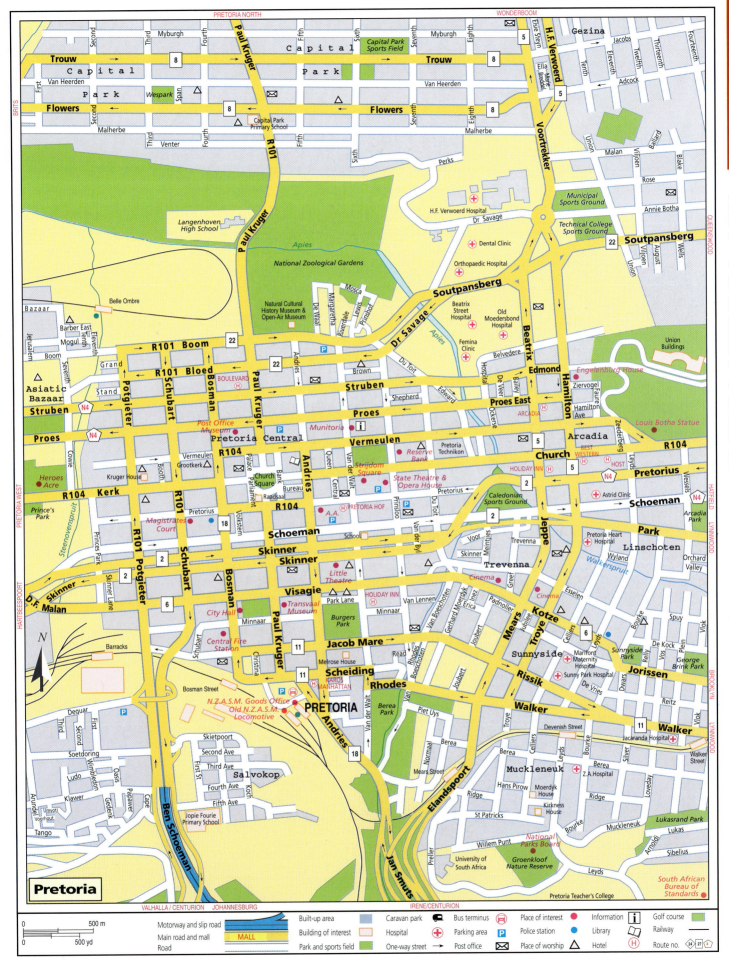

KEY TOURIST AREAS

Pretoria

Motorway and slip road	Built-up area
Main road and mall	Building of interest
Road	Park and sports field
	Caravan park
	Hospital
	One-way street

Bus terminus	Place of interest
Parking area	Police station
Post office	Library
Place of worship	Golf course
Hotel	Railway
	Route no.

PILANESBERG AND SUN CITY

*T*he dramatic Lost City and Sun City leisure resort, one of South Africa's most glittering tourist venues featuring casinos, bars, restaurants, theatres, nightclubs and shops, is set among the lush vegetation of beautifully landscaped grounds, in what before was little more than desert territory. Apart from the 31,500m² (339,063ft²) Valley of the Waves, a man-made water park with soft sand beaches, waterslides, cascades and 1.8m-high (5.9ft) waves, the complex also offers an Arizona Desert-style golf course where crocodiles lie in wait at the 13th hole, and another at the Gary Player Country Club, venue of the annual Million Dollar Golf Challenge.

Pilanesberg National Park north of Sun City has some 10,000 head of wildlife including the Big Five – buffalo, rhino (black and white), elephant, lion and leopard – and over 300 bird species. This game-rich habitat lies within four concentric mountain rings, the relics of an ancient volcano. In the centre of the bowl is Mankwe Lake, a favourite hippo haunt. The park is traversed by a network of game-viewing roads; guided walks and drives are conducted and hot-air balloon trips can be organized. This wonderful park is the result of 'Operation Genesis', a successful game-stocking venture. A visit to the aviary at Manyane Gate should not be missed.

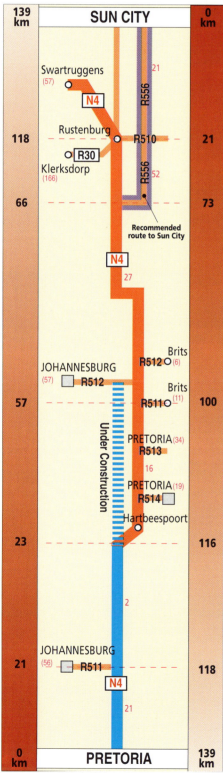

ACCOMMODATION

Sun City complex
tel: (01465) 2-1000, fax: 2-1470.
The Cascades ★★★★★, opulent.
Palace of the Lost City ★★★★★, the ultimate in luxurious extravagance and splendour.
Sun City Cabanas ★★★, mainly family-oriented and affordable.
Sun City Main Hotel ★★★★★, superb five-star comfort.
Pilanesberg National Park
Bakubung Game Lodge ★★★★, tel: (01465) 2-1861, fax: 2-1621; thatched rooms around a hippo pool in a private game reserve.
Kwa Maritane Game Lodge ★★★★, tel: (01465) 2-1820, fax: 2-1268; luxurious accommodation in the African bush.

SUN CITY	J	F	M	A	M	J	J	A	S	O	N	D
AV. TEMP. °C	23	23	21	18	15	12	12	14	18	21	22	23
AV. TEMP. °F	73	73	70	64	59	54	54	57	64	70	72	73
DAILY SUN hrs	8	8	8	7	9	9	9	10	10	9	8	9
RAINFALL mm	138	98	76	57	17	8	5	7	17	53	98	111
RAINFALL in	5.5	4	3	2.5	0.7	0.3	0.2	0.3	0.7	2.5	4	4.5

USEFUL CONTACTS

Pilanesberg National Park, tel: (01465) 5-5356; for the real bush experience.
Sun International Group Central Reservations, tel: (011) 780-7443.

DISTANCE IN KM FROM SUN CITY	
Johannesburg	173
Pretoria	139
Rustenburg	48

Below: *The Palace of the Lost City rises dramatically out of the surrounding African bush, like the legendary temple of a mysterious civilization.*

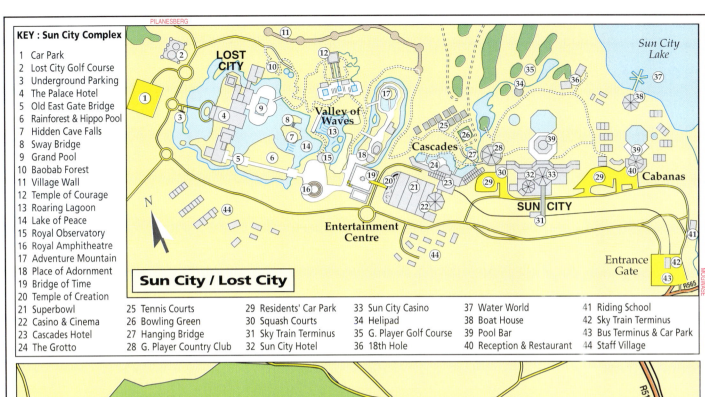

KEY : Sun City Complex

1 Car Park
2 Lost City Golf Course
3 Underground Parking
4 The Palace Hotel
5 Old East Gate Bridge
6 Rainforest & Hippo Pool
7 Hidden Cave Falls
8 Sway Bridge
9 Grand Pool
10 Baobab Forest
11 Village Wall
12 Temple of Courage
13 Roaring Lagoon
14 Lake of Peace
15 Royal Observatory
16 Royal Amphitheatre
17 Adventure Mountain
18 Place of Adornment
19 Bridge of Time
20 Temple of Creation
21 Superbowl
22 Casino & Cinema
23 Cascades Hotel
24 The Grotto

25 Tennis Courts
26 Bowling Green
27 Hanging Bridge
28 G. Player Country Club

29 Residents' Car Park
30 Squash Courts
31 Sky Train Terminus
32 Sun City Hotel

33 Sun City Casino
34 Helipad
35 G. Player Golf Course
36 18th Hole

37 Water World
38 Boat House
39 Pool Bar
40 Reception & Restaurant

41 Riding School
42 Sky Train Terminus
43 Bus Terminus & Car Park
44 Staff Village

Sun City / Lost City

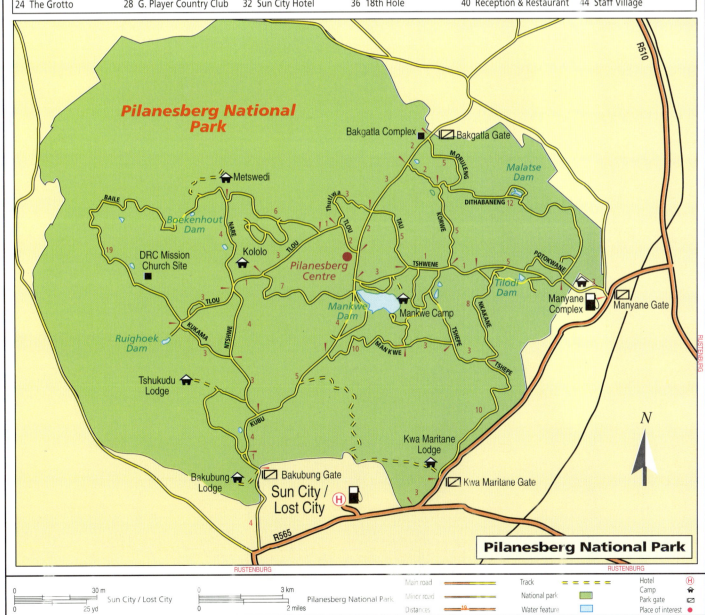

Pilanesberg National Park

0	30 m		0	3 km
0	25 yd	Sun City / Lost City	0	2 miles	Pilanesberg National Park

Main road		Track	
Minor road		National park	
Distances 19		Water feature	
		Hotel (H)	
		Camp	
		Park gate	
		Place of interest ●	

KEY TOURIST AREAS

KRUGER NATIONAL PARK

South Africa's premier wildlife sanctuary covers more than 20,000 km² (7720 sq miles) – an area about the size of Wales and larger than the state of Israel. Because this vast, wild expanse encompasses many different habitats, it is a haven for more varieties of wildlife than any other game reserve in Africa. Among the approximately 140 mammal species occurring here are the Big Five: lion (approximately 1500), elephant (about 8000), leopard (around 1000), buffalo (25,000), and rhino, both black and white. Other large wildlife populations include zebra, wildebeest, giraffe, hippo and crocodile, as well as some 500 bird species. If you are lucky, you may even spot a pack of the increasingly rare wild dogs.

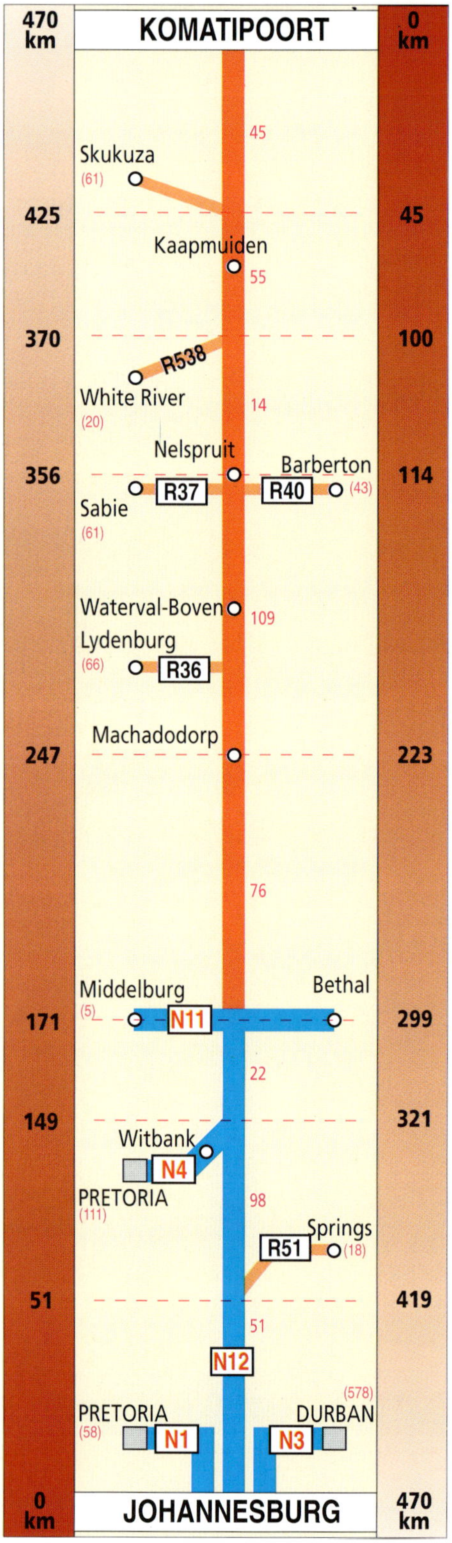

TRAVEL TIPS

An extensive network, consisting of about 880km (550 miles) of tarred surface and 1700km (1060 miles) of gravel road, traverses the park, providing effective access to all areas of the Kruger.

Should you experience any car trouble, vehicle breakdown services are available at Skukuza and Letaba camps.

A few general safety guidelines have to be observed by all visitors :

- Malaria treatment should be started prior to entering this area (consult your physician), and use insect repellent.
- Stay on the designated roads or tracks.
- Keep to the speed limit.
- Do not leave your vehicle.
- Don't injure, feed or disturb wildlife.
- Littering is an offence.
- Be sure to arrive at your rest camp by the stipulated time before sunset.

DISTANCE IN KM TO KRUGER NATIONAL PARK	
Bloemfontein	823
Cape Town	1827
Durban	780
Johannesburg	425
Port Elizabeth	1500

MAIN ATTRACTIONS

Olifants Camp: dramatically perched on a clifftop; the park's most magnificent viewing-point over the game-rich valley below.

Letaba Elephant Museum: an interesting exhibition at this camp.

Private game lodges: though generally very expensive, **Mala-Mala** (voted one of the world's finest safari destinations), **Sabi Sabi** and **Londolozi** are the ultimate in bushveld luxury.

Nwanetsi Lookout Point: magnificent viewpoint overlooking the Sweni River.

Mmphongolo drive: one of the best in the northern region.

Pafuri: in the far north is the best place in the park to view birds; superb scenery with a high density of baobab trees.

Stephenson-Hamilton Library: in Skukuza; interesting displays.

Night drives: well worth the cost; you may even spot a leopard.

Tshokwane Picnic Spot: highly recommended rest-stop where refreshments can be purchased.

ACCOMMODATION

Over 20 pleasant, clean and safe rest camps are located within the park. For all enquiries, contact the **National Parks Board: Pretoria**, tel: (012) 343-1991; **Cape Town**, tel: (021) 22-2810.

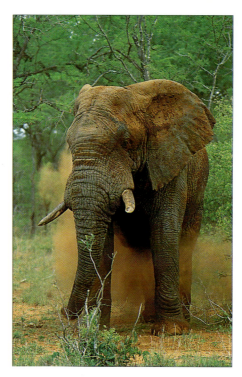

Left: *Elephants should always be approached with caution. Displays of aggression such as a raised trunk and flapping ears should never be underestimated.*

Route map (left column)

KOMATIPOORT — 470 km / 0 km

- Skukuza (61) — 45
- 425 km / 45 km
- Kaapmuiden — 55
- 370 km / 100 km
- R538 — White River (20) — 14
- Nelspruit — 356 km
- R37 — Barberton — R40 (43) — 114 km
- Sabie (61)
- Waterval-Boven — 109
- Lydenburg (66) — R36
- Machadodorp — 247 km / 223 km
- 76
- Middelburg (5) — N11 — Bethal — 171 km / 299 km
- 22
- 149 km / 321 km
- Witbank — N4
- PRETORIA (111) — 98
- R51 — Springs (18)
- 51 km / 419 km
- 51
- N12
- PRETORIA (58) — N1 — (578) — DURBAN — N3
- **JOHANNESBURG** — 0 km / 470 km

SATARA	J	F	M	A	M	J	J	A	S	O	N	D
AV. TEMP. °C	27	27	25	23	19	17	16	19	21	24	24	26
AV. TEMP. °F	81	81	77	73	66	63	61	66	70	75	75	79
DAILY SUN hrs	7	8	7	7	8	8	8	8	8	7	6	7
RAINFALL mm	51	91	42	25	7	15	8	9	16	38	59	76
RAINFALL in	2.5	4	2	1	0.3	0.6	0.3	0.3	0.6	1.5	2.5	3

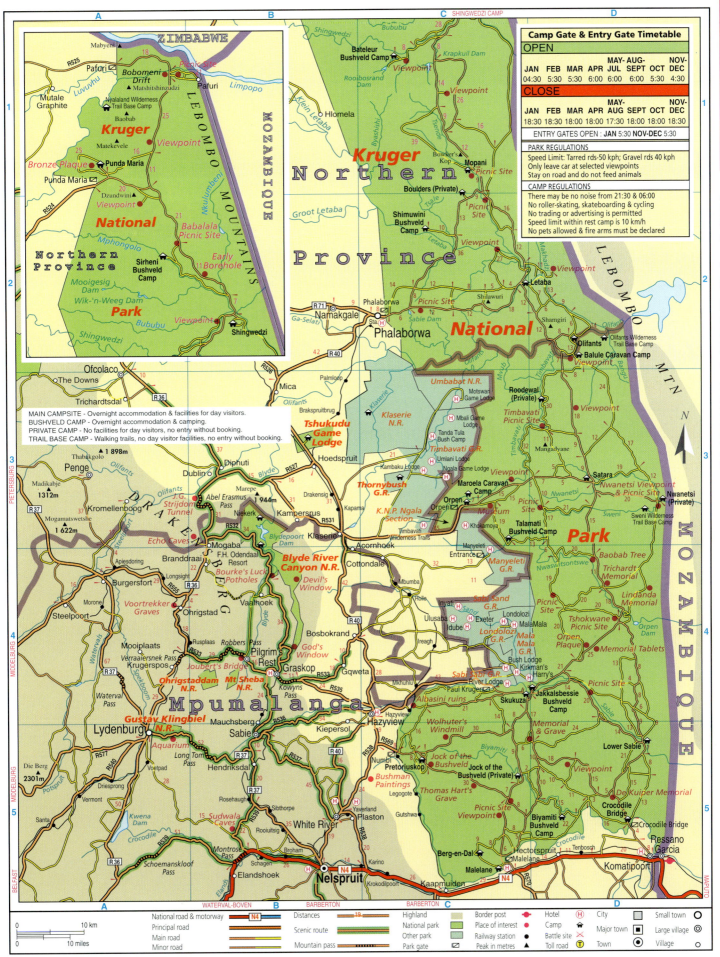

KEY TOURIST AREAS

Camp Gate & Entry Gate Timetable

OPEN				MAY-AUG-		NOV-
JAN	FEB	MAR	APR	JUL SEPT OCT		DEC
04:30	5:30	5:30	6:00	6:00 6:00 5:30		4:30

CLOSE				MAY-		NOV-
JAN	FEB	MAR	APR	AUG SEPT OCT		DEC
18:30	18:30	18:00	18:00	17:30 18:00 18:00		18:30

ENTRY GATES OPEN : JAN 5:30 NOV-DEC 5:30

PARK REGULATIONS
Speed Limit: Tarred rds-50 kph; Gravel rds 40 kph
Only leave car at selected viewpoints
Stay on road and do not feed animals

CAMP REGULATIONS
There may be no noise from 21:30 & 06:00
No roller-skating, skateboarding & cycling
No trading or advertising is permitted
Speed limit within rest camp is 10 km/h
No pets allowed & fire arms must be declared

MAIN CAMPSITE - Overnight accommodation & facilities for day visitors.
BUSHVELD CAMP - Overnight accommodation & camping.
PRIVATE CAMP - No facilities for day visitors, no entry without booking.
TRAIL BASE CAMP - Walking trails, no day visitor facilities, no entry without booking.

National road & motorway — N4
Principal road
Main road
Minor road

Distances — 19
Scenic route
Mountain pass

Highland
National park
Other park
Park gate

Border post
Place of interest
Railway station
Peak in metres

Hotel
Camp
Battle site
Toll road — T

City — H
Major town
Town

Small town
Large village
Village

0   10 km
0   10 miles

MPUMALANGA

*M*ountainous terrain, misty forests, bushveld and endless views are the compelling features of this escarpment region far to the east of Gauteng, across the great Highveld plateau. For sheer scenic beauty, few parts of the southern African subcontinent can compare with the Great Escarpment, a spectacular wonderland of buttresses, strangely sculpted peaks and deep ravines. The Olifants and Crocodile rivers and a score of their tributaries run through verdant valleys. One tributary, the Blyde River, over centuries carved a canyon that now ranks as one of Africa's great scenic splendours.

MAIN ATTRACTIONS

Blyde River Canyon: a majestic gorge whose sheer cliff faces plunge to the water far below.
Bourke's Luck Potholes: a fantasia of hollowed-out rocks.
Pilgrim's Rest: town born out of the 1870 gold rush, now a quaint, living museum.
Jock of the Bushveld: plaques along former Lowveld transport routes commemorate this heroic dog, immortalized in the classic novel by Sir Percy FitzPatrick.
God's Window: for the most magnificent views of the area.
Mount Sheba: beautiful forest reserve high in the mountains.
Tzaneen: attractive town in the heart of the fertile Letaba district.
Magoebaskloof: large tracts of thick indigenous forest.
Long Tom Pass: spectacular pass between Sabie and Lydenburg.
Echo Caves: archaeological evidence of earlier inhabitants.

TRAVEL TIPS

The region has an excellent network of roads. Travelling from Johannesburg to Nelspruit and the escarpment, take the R22 and then the N4 near Witbank; from Pretoria take the N4 direct. The R40 leads from Nelspruit north into the escarpment. To reach the northern and northeastern territory, follow the N1 national highway from Pretoria; turn right at Pietersburg on the R71 for Tzaneen and the central region of the Kruger National Park (around Phalaborwa). If you intend travelling into the far northern region of the park, take the R524 at Louis Trichardt. Please note: this is a **malaria** area so ensure that the necessary precautions are taken before travelling into this area; alternatively consult your physician for advice.

ACCOMMODATION

Mount Sheba Hotel ★★★★, west of Pilgrim's Rest, tel: (013) 768-1241, fax: 768-1248; luxury hotel.
Sabi River Sun ★★★★, close to Paul Kruger Gate, tel: (013) 737-7311, fax: 737-7314; 18-hole golf course.
Pine Lake Sun ★★★★, White River, tel: (013) 751-5036, fax: 751-5134; on the edge of a lake; golf course.
Royal Hotel, Pilgrim's Rest, tel: (013) 768-1100, fax: 768-1188; for an unforgettable stay in a national monument; charming accommodation in authentic tin-roofed houses with antique furnishings.

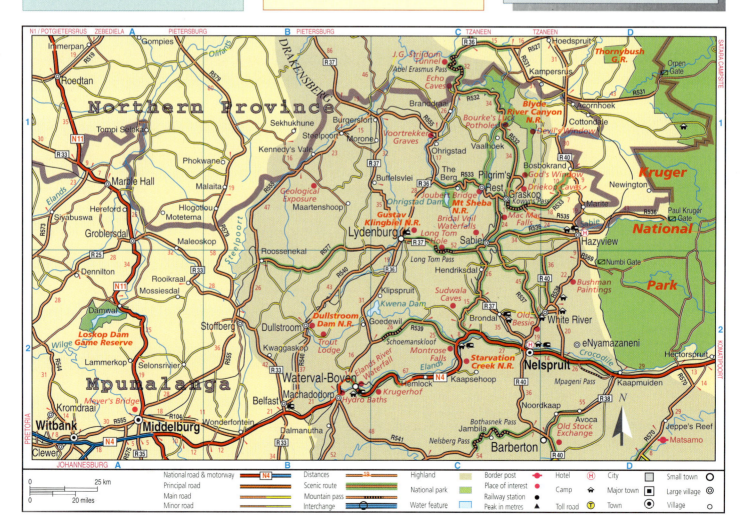

NELSPRUIT

The hot dry plains below the Great Escarpment are known as the Lowveld. The largest town in this grassland region of Mpumalanga and situated on the banks of the Crocodile River, Nelspruit is the centre of a fertile and beautiful agricultural area. It is an attractive and prosperous town of wide streets lined with poinciana trees that are ablaze with deep red blossoms during the summer months. This is the last major town en route to the Kruger National Park. Among Nelspruit's attractions are good hotels and restaurants, sophisticated shops and speciality outlets.

ACCOMMODATION

Cybele Forest Lodge ★★★★, on the R40, White River, tel: (013) 764-1823, fax: 764-1810; exclusive retreat surrounded by nature.
Hotel The Winkler ★★★★, tel: (013) 751-5068, fax: 751-5044; in the beautiful White River area.
Paragon Hotel ★★★, 19 Anderson Street, tel/fax: (013) 753-3205; pleasant, clean and comfortable.
Fig Tree Hotel ★★, 16 Anderson Street, tel: (013) 752-2955, fax: 753-3205; convenient location.
Lowveld Lodge, Kastings Street, White River, tel: (013) tel/fax: 750-0206; self-catering chalets.

MAIN ATTRACTIONS

Lowveld Botanic Gardens: on the banks of the Crocodile River, supporting over 500 indigenous species of flora.
Lowveld Herbarium: adjacent to the Gardens; of interest to the botanist as well as the layperson.
Sudwala Caves: dramatic cave formations and an interesting dinosaur park, about 40km (25 miles) northwest of Nelspruit.
Riverside Trail: self-guided 4km (2½-mile) hike along the Crocodile River, with some lovely waterfalls.
Farmstalls: roadside stalls around the town sell fresh fruit and curios.

WATERFALL ROUTE

There are several beautiful waterfalls in the Sabie/Graskop area some 50km (31 miles) north of Nelspruit. A visit to the waterfalls makes a lovely excursion, all of them are easily accessible; the roads are generally in very good condition, although dense fog patches may occur. Among the best falls to view are:
Bridal Veil: a delicate spray of water surrounded by a forest echoing with the call of many birds; 7km (4.2 miles) north of Sabie.
Mac-Mac: twin cascades plunge 56m (185ft) into a deep, green ravine.
Lone Creek: hidden some 68m (222ft) in a beautiful, misty forest.
Horseshoe: a national monument.
Berlin: plunges about 48m (158ft) into a deep pool.
Lisbon: picturesque double waterfall in a setting of special beauty.

USEFUL CONTACTS

Rob Ferreira Hospital, tel: (013) 741-3031.
Nelspruit Publicity, tel: (013) 755-1988.
Mpumalanga Tourist Board, tel: (013) 752-7001/2/3; tourist information.

KEY TOURIST AREAS

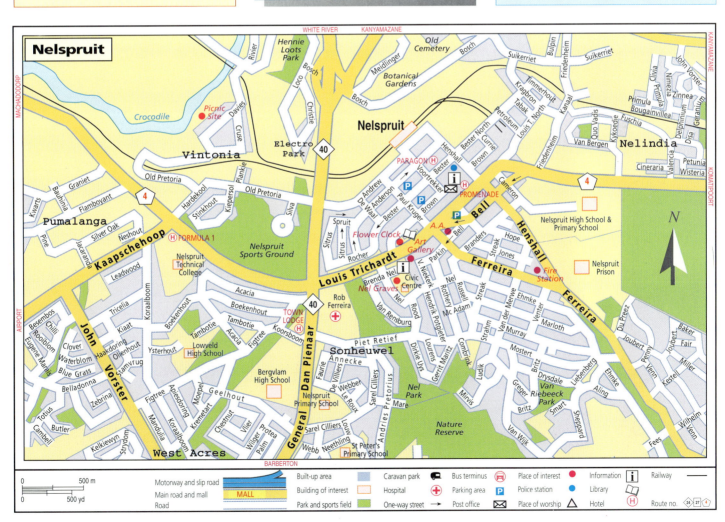

KWAZULU-NATAL NORTH COAST

*R*emarkable for its rich fauna and flora, northern KwaZulu-Natal boasts some of South Africa's finest game reserves (among them the Hluhluwe/Umfolozi Park, oldest of South Africa's many wildlife sanctuaries) and one of the world's great wetland and marine sanctuaries, the Greater St Lucia Wetland Park. Just north of Durban, along the Dolphin Coast that stretches for 90km (55 miles) up to the Tugela River mouth, lies the upmarket resort town of Umhlanga Rocks. Beyond lies the area historically known as Zululand, where Richards Bay is the largest city and industrial hub due to its deep-water port (the busiest in the country). The broad beaches, fringed by lush, tropical vegetation, attract sunbathers, anglers, divers and boating enthusiasts.

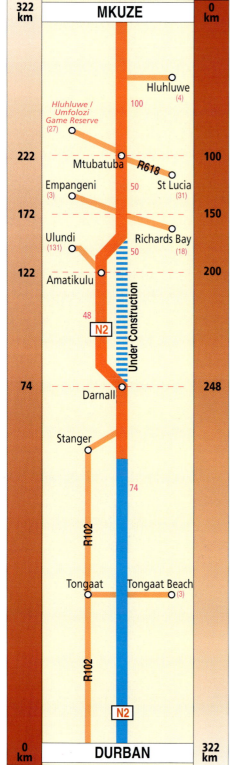

MAIN ATTRACTIONS

Beaches: some of the country's finest beaches are to be found north of Durban. These include Umhlanga Rocks, Tongaat, Ballito, Shaka's Rock, Salt Rock, Shelly Beach, North Beach (Margate) and Uvongo.

Natal Sharks Board: in Umhlanga; maybe witness the dissection of a shark and enjoy an informative audio-visual presentation.

Lake Sibaya: South Africa's largest natural freshwater lake.

The Greater St Lucia Wetland Park: many beautiful lakes, swamps, forests and marshlands surround the fauna-rich, shallow-water estuary of Lake St Lucia.

Maputaland Reserves: host some of the greatest concentrations of wildlife in the entire country.

The **Hluhluwe/Umfolozi Park** is famed for its rhino conservation programme and offers a haven for the Big Five.

Phinda Resource Reserve: luxury lodge, one of the best ecotourism destinations in the country.

Sodwana Bay: pristine marine wonderland, the best diving venue in the country.

Shakaland: model of a traditional Zulu village in the Nkwaleni Valley. Attractions here include culinary specialities, tribal dancing and traditional healers.

DISTANCE IN KM FROM ST LUCIA	
Durban	253
Hluhluwe/Umfolozi Park	58
Johannesburg	633

RICHARDS BAY	J	F	M	A	M	J	J	A	S	O	N	D
AV. TEMP. °C	25	25	25	23	20	18	17	19	20	21	23	25
AV. TEMP. °F	77	77	77	73	68	64	63	66	68	70	73	77
DAILY SUN hrs	7	7	7	8	8	7	8	8	7	6	7	7
RAINFALL mm	144	138	110	111	126	31	47	59	84	97	97	83
RAINFALL in	6	5.5	4.5	4.5	5	1	2	2.5	3.5	4	4	3.5
SEA TEMP. °C	24	24	24	23	22	21	20	20	20	21	21	23
SEA TEMP. °F	75	75	75	73	72	70	68	68	68	70	70	73

TRAVEL TIPS

The N2 runs parallel to, but out of sight of, the coast to the general vicinity of Richards Bay (about 2½ hours' drive north of Durban), and then sweeps inland to the Swaziland border. Major roads in Zululand are tarred; most of the minor ones (including those in the game reserves) are gravel and generally in a satisfactory condition.

USEFUL CONTACTS

Dolphin Coast Publicity Association, tel: (0322) 6-1997.
Isle of Capri, tel: (031) 37-7751, fax: 466-2434; offer educational tours, 1-hour deep-sea cruises, 1½-hour dinner-dance cruises and deep-sea fishing trips.
Natal Parks Board, Pietermaritzburg, tel: (0331) 47-1981.
Tourism KwaZulu-Natal, tel: (031) 304-7144.
Umhlanga Publicity, tel: (031) 561-4257.

Right: *The golden sands of St Lucia, washed by the warm Indian Ocean, make this a popular spot with watersports enthusiasts and sunbathers.*

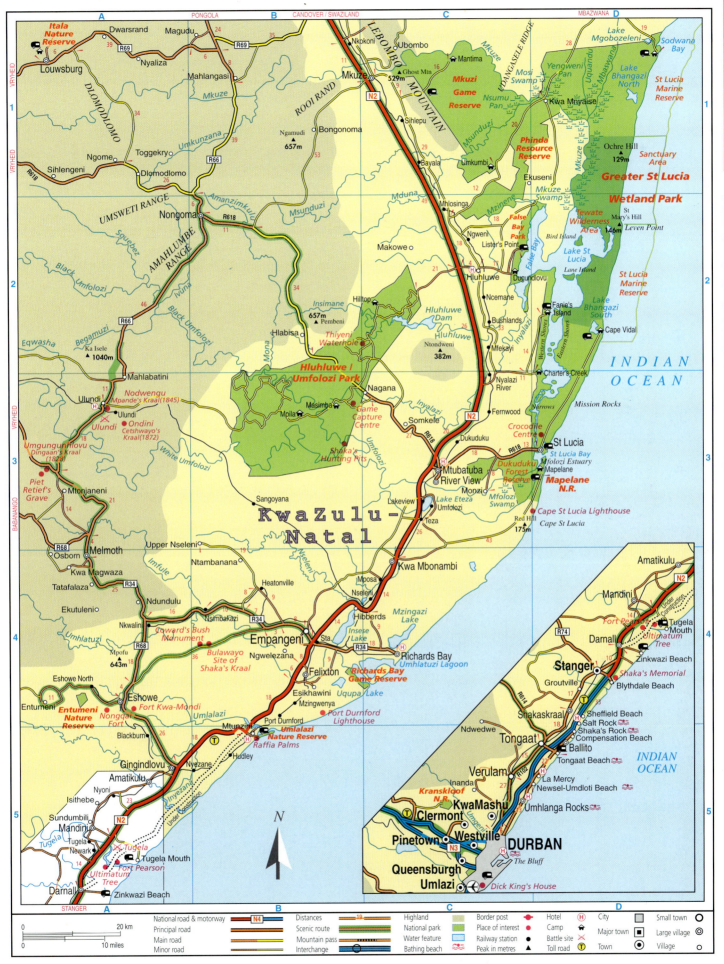

KEY TOURIST AREAS

KWAZULU-NATAL SOUTH COAST

*T*he southern coast of KwaZulu-Natal is a lush tropical wonderland of wide, unspoilt beaches lapped by the warm aquamarine waters of the Indian Ocean. A string of friendly little towns and hamlets, each with its own attractions, lines this wonderful coastline, offering accommodation and a selection of restaurants. Although there is no visible distinction, the coast south of Durban is divided into two sections: the area from Amanzimtoti, just south of Durban, to Mtwalume is known as the Sunshine Coast, that from Hibberdene to Port Edward is called the Hibiscus Coast; both offer outstanding holiday venues.

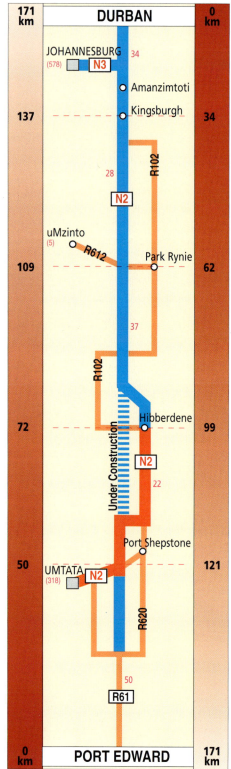

MAIN ATTRACTIONS

Sunshine Coast
Kingsburgh: five seaside resorts popular for their white sands and shark-protected bathing.
Umkomaas: a championship golf course and floodlit tidal pool.
Scottburgh: a charming beach, and fascinating Crocworld nearby.
Vernon Crookes Nature Reserve: lush sanctuary for various antelope.

Hibiscus Coast
Hibberdene: lagoon, woodland-fringed beaches, amusement park.
uMzumbe: excellent family hotel; rock and surf angling.
Banana Beach: safe bathing and very good surfing.
Bendigo: four seaside resorts geared towards holiday-makers.

Umtentweni: for a quiet getaway.
Port Shepstone: at the mouth of the Umzimkulu River; offers excellent bowling greens and one of South Africa's best golf courses.
Oribi Gorge Nature Reserve: some 20km (14 miles) inland from Port Shepstone – a striking canyon carved through layers of sandstone by the Umzimkulwana River.
Uvongo: lively little resort in an idyllic tropical setting.
Margate: very popular seaside town, but it can get crowded.
Ramsgate: magnificent lagoon and a long beach.
Port Edward: charming town in the former Transkei, with a pleasant beach; close to the Wild Coast Sun.

Above: *Scottburgh is a popular holiday resort on the Sunshine Coast. The lovely beach offers safe bathing, as well as some fine angling spots.*

USEFUL CONTACTS

Hospital GJ Crookes, Scottburgh, tel: (0323) 2-1300.
Hibiscus Coast Publicity Association, Margate, tel: (03931) 2-2322.
Sunshine Coast Publicity Association, Scottburgh, tel: (0323) 2-1364.

TRAVEL TIPS

Towns and resorts are linked to Durban by the N2 as far as Port Shepstone, while the R61 leads to Port Edward. Both roads are in good condition, though inland roads can be a little rough and caution is advised.

DISTANCE IN KM FROM PORT SHEPSTONE	
Durban	121
Richards Bay	311
Umtata	312

KEY TOURIST AREAS

DURBAN AND PIETERMARITZBURG

*T*he city of Durban is the country's third-largest metropolis, and its foremost seaport (in fact, it has the biggest and busiest harbour in Africa). With its fine beaches and tourist amenities, Durban is a popular holiday destination in South Africa, especially due to its excellent watersports facilities: its beaches offer some of the best surfing venues in the country, and deep-sea game-fishing trips, scuba diving and sailing trips are all readily available to the tourist.

ACCOMMODATION

Royal Hotel ★★★★★, 267 Smith Street, tel: (031) 304-0331, fax: 307-6884; one of the best, offering luxury and excellent service.
Holiday Inn Crowne Plaza Durban ★★★★, 63 Snell Parade, tel: (031) 37-1321, fax: 332-5527; large resort hotel with an international business centre; three restaurants and two bars.
Beach Hotel ★★★, Marine Parade, tel: (031) 37-5511, fax: 37-5409; conveniently situated on the Golden Mile beachfront.
Holiday Inn Garden Court (Marine Parade) ★★★, next to the Edward Hotel, tel: (031) 37-3341, fax: 37-5929; stylish and comfortable, with reliable service.
Balmoral Hotel, 125 Marine Parade, tel: (031) 368-5940, fax: 368-5955; situated right across the road from the beach.
Sandhurst Hotel, 202 Currie Road, tel: (031) 21-4241, fax: 21-4243; a 78-room hotel, located 5km (3 miles) from the beach on the bus route.

USEFUL CONTACTS

Addington Hospital, tel: (031) 332-2111.
Sea Rescue Services, tel: (031) 37-2200.
Durban Tourism, Tourist Junction Building, tel: (031) 304-4934.
SATOUR, tel: (031) 305-2091.
Timeless Afrika (run by the Zululand–Thukela Marketing Authority), tel: (031) 307-3800, fax: 307-3822.
Sea World and the Oceanographic Research Centre, tel: (031) 37-3536; for information about show times.
Sarie Marais **Cruises**, tel: (031) 305-4022, fax: 25-8788; offer interesting harbour and dinner-dance cruises.

DURBAN	J	F	M	A	M	J	J	A	S	O	N	D
AV. TEMP. °C	24	25	24	22	19	17	16	17	19	20	22	23
AV. TEMP. °F	75	77	75	72	66	63	61	63	66	68	72	73
DAILY SUN hrs	6	7	7	7	7	7	7	7	6	5	5	6
RAINFALL mm	135	114	124	87	64	26	44	58	65	89	104	108
RAINFALL in	5.5	4.5	5	3.5	3	1	2	2.5	3	4	4.5	4.5
SEA TEMP. °C	24	25	24	23	21	20	19	19	20	21	22	23
SEA TEMP. °F	75	77	75	73	70	68	66	66	68	70	72	73

Below: *The Paddling Pools form part of Durban's sparkling Golden Mile which is lined with colourful markets, many restaurants, walkways and fountains.*

MAIN ATTRACTIONS

Golden Mile: fabulous holiday playground stretching for 6km (4 miles) along the sandy Indian Ocean shoreline, with everything the entertainment-seeking tourist could desire.
Pietermaritzburg: quaint colonial-style town with fine architecture and very interesting museums.
Sea World: on the Golden Mile, popular aquarium–dolphinarium.
Fitzsimon's Snake Park: home to many indigenous and exotic species, as well as crocodiles.
Victoria Street Indian Market: colourful and exotic place of bargain and barter, housed in a huge domed building.
Umgeni River Bird Park: rated third best of the world's bird parks; has approximately 300 local and exotic species.
Mahatma Gandhi Museum: dedicated to the memory of this great leader.
The Wheel: very lively and glitzy modern shopping complex, with many tempting restaurants and live entertainment.
Port Natal Maritime Museum: on the Victoria Embankment; interesting exhibits for young and old.

TRAVEL TIPS

Durban is linked to all other major South African centres by a network of national roads. The N2 leads south and then east along the coast, through Port Elizabeth to Cape Town. The N3 takes the traveller northwest through Pietermaritzburg and Harrismith to Johannesburg.

Events and Festivals

Durban International Film Festival: held in **January**.
Comrades Marathon: famous marathon in **June** (Durban to Pietermaritzburg the one year, vice versa the following one).
Rothman's July Handicap: prestigious horseracing event in **July**.
Gunston 500: world-renowned annual surfing contest held in the Bay of Plenty in **July**.

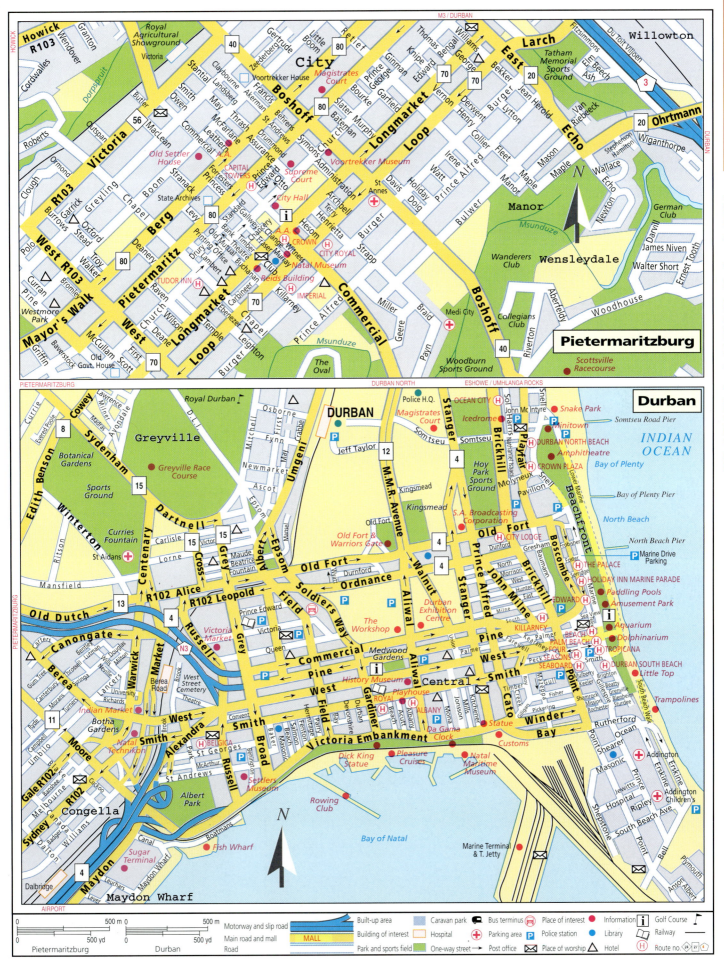

KEY TOURIST AREAS

Pietermaritzburg

Durban

INDIAN OCEAN

Bay of Plenty

North Beach

Bay of Natal

Scale	
Pietermaritzburg	Durban

Motorway and slip road
Main road and mall
MALL
Road

Built-up area
Building of interest
Park and sports field

Caravan park
Hospital
One-way street

Bus terminus
Parking area
Police station
Post office

Place of interest
Information
Library
Place of worship

Golf Course
Railway
Hotel
Route no.

DRAKENSBERG MOUNTAIN RESORTS

South Africa's highest mountain range, the Drakensberg is a massive and strikingly beautiful rampart of deep gorges, pinnacles and saw-edged ridges, caves, overhangs and balancing rocks. In the winter months its upper levels lie deep in snow, but clustered among the foothills far below, in undulating grassland, is a score of resort hotels created and maintained for family holiday-makers. People come for the fresh, clean mountain air; for the walks, climbs and drives; for the gentler sports (trout fishing, golf, bowls and horseback riding); and for casual relaxation in the most exquisite surrounds. Particularly recommended are the northern (Mont-Aux-Sources) and central Drakensberg areas (Giant's Castle to Cathedral Peak).

ACCOMMODATION

Cathedral Peak Hotel ★★★, Winterton, tel/fax: (036) 488-1888; set amid some spectacular peaks.
Drakensberg Sun Hotel ★★★, in the central Drakensberg region, tel: (036) 468-1000, fax: 468-1224; wonderful views.

Little Switzerland Hotel ★★★, between Bergville and Harrismith, tel: (036) 438-6220, fax: 438-6222; view of the spectacular Amphitheatre.
Sani Pass Hotel ★★★, Himeville, tel: (033) 702-1320, fax: 702-0220; 800ha (1977 acres) at the foot of Sani Pass.

Champagne Castle, tel: (036) 468-1063, fax: 468-1306; guided walks; golf course.
Royal Natal National Park Hotel, Mont-Aux-Sources, tel: (036) 438-6200, fax: 438-6101; beautiful hiking resort in a lovely setting.

MAIN ATTRACTIONS

Royal Natal National Park: an extensive and beautiful floral and wildlife sanctuary. Excursions are offered to the imposing Mont-Aux-Sources plateau and its giant, natural Amphitheatre, as well as to the spectacular Tugela Falls, the country's highest waterfall.
Giant's Castle Game Reserve: in the central Drakensberg, dominated by the Giant's Castle and Injesuthi buttresses, a scenic wonderland famous for its Bushman rock art and raptor conservation programmes.
Ndedema Gorge: 'place of rolling thunder'; a magnificent gorge renowned for its rock art.
Himeville Nature Reserve: in the southern Drakensberg; a paradise for trout fishermen.
Drakensberg Boys Choir School: in the foothills of beautiful Champagne Castle; the world-famous choir performs for the public on Wednesday afternoons.

USEFUL CONTACTS

Mountain Rescue Club (via the Natal Parks Board – stationed at Monk's Cowl), tel: (036) 468-1103.
Basotho Cultural Village, Witsieshoek, tel: (05861) 31794.
Drakensberg Tourism, tel: (036) 448-1557.
Drakensberg Boys Choir School, tel: (036) 468-1012, except during school holidays.
Wildways Mountaineering & Guiding Services, Mooiriver, tel: (0333) 3-7496.

Below: Impressive Giant's Castle, just one of the spectacular formations to be found in the beautiful Drakensberg Mountain range.

Route map (JOHANNESBURG to DURBAN)

578 km	JOHANNESBURG	0 km
	Nigel (12)	
(2) Heidelberg	121	
457	Villiers	121
	153	
304	Harrismith **N5**	274
	Bethlehem	
	35	
269	Van Reenen	309
	Ladysmith **N11** (20)	
	R616	
	Bergville	
The Natal Drakensberg Park	104 **R74**	
165	Estcourt	413
The Natal Drakensberg Park	86	
	Mooi River	
	Howick	
79	PIETERMARITZBURG	499
The Natal Drakensberg Park	**N3**	
	79	
0 km	DURBAN	578 km

ESTCOURT	J	F	M	A	M	J	J	A	S	O	N	D
AV. TEMP. °C	21	21	20	17	13	10	11	13	16	18	19	21
AV. TEMP. °F	70	70	68	63	55	50	52	55	61	64	66	70
DAILY SUN hrs	7	7	7	7	8	8	9	9	8	7	7	7
RAINFALL mm	147	87	74	47	10	6	6	26	37	66	94	129
RAINFALL in	6	3.5	3	2	0.4	0.2	0.2	1	1.5	3	4	5.5

Free State

KwaZulu-Natal

LESOTHO

Harrismith

Phuthaditjhaba

Northern Berg Resorts

Sterkfontein Dam N.R.

Rugged Glen N.R.

Royal Natal National Park

Little Switzerland

The Cavern Berg Resort

Mont-Aux-Sources Hotel

Spioenkop Dam N.R.

Bergville

Cathedral Peak Hotel

Cathkin Park Hotel

Ndedema Gorge

Champagne Castle Hotel

Dragon Peaks

Central Berg Resorts

White Mountain Resort

Wagendrift N.R.

Weenen G.R.

Ladysmith

Colenso

Estcourt

Mooi River

Giant's Castle

The Natal Drakensberg Park

Rosetta

Nottingham Road

Craigieburn N.R.

Umgeni Vlei N.R.

Howick

Karkloof N.R.

Midmar Public Resort N.R.

Albert Falls Public Resort N.R.

Queen Elizabeth N.P.

PIETERMARITZBURG

Edendale

Natal Lion Park

Himeville N.R.

Coleford N.R.

Sehlabathebe National Park

Drakensberg Garden Hotel

Bushman's Nek Hotel

Underberg

National road & motorway	Distances	Highland	Border post	Hotel	City	Small town
Principal road	Scenic route	National park	Place of interest	Camp	Major town	Large village
Main road	Mountain pass	Water feature	Railway station	Battle site	Town	Village
Minor road	Interchange	Lodge / resort	Nest	Peak in metres	Toll road	

0   20 km

0   10 miles

31

HISTORIC BATTLEFIELDS

For most of the 19th century, the KwaZulu-Natal midlands region was a bloody battlefield, as Zulu, Boer and Briton fought for territorial supremacy. Military enthusiasts – indeed anyone interested in the region's turbulent past – will find the Battlefields Route (which includes the sites of Blood River, Isandhlwana, Rorke's Drift, Ulundi, Majuba Hill, Talana, Elandslaagte, Tugela Heights, Colenso, Ladysmith and Spioenkop) fascinating. Some of the most dramatic confrontations occurred in the triangular area bounded by Estcourt in the south, Volksrust in the north, and Vryheid to the east.

TRAVEL TIPS

Tour by Greyhound coach or embark on self-guided drives (Walk 'n Talk audio cassettes available). Call the local publicity association or the curator of the **Talana Museum**, tel: (0341) 2-2654, for information.

THE BATTLE ROUTE

Blood River (1838): the final and decisive clash between the Zulus and the Voortrekker pioneers during the Boer migration into Natal. Raw courage proved no match for superior firepower – more than 3000 Zulus perished on the field; the Boer losses amounted to three wounded.

Isandhlwana (1879): part of a British invading force, under Lord Chelmsford's overall command, was annihilated by 24,000 Zulu *impi* (warriors); only a handful of the 1000-plus redcoats survived.

Rorke's Drift (1879): a bitterly fought skirmish in which a small British garrison held out against wave after wave of Zulu *impi*. This dramatic battle was much publicized by the British press; between them, the defenders earned 11 Victoria Crosses.

Majuba Hill (1881): final battle of the brief Anglo-Transvaal war, in which a Boer force of part-time soldiers drove the British regulars from the slopes of the high hill, inflicting severe casualties. The British commander, Sir George Colley, is thought to have committed suicide during the retreat.

Spioenkop (1991): the Anglo-Boer War's bloodiest battle, savagely fought between Boer and Briton for control of the strategic hill on the route leading to the besieged Ladysmith. Casualties were high on both sides; the Boers eventually prevailed.

WILD COAST

J̲ust South of Port Edward, between the Umtamvuna River and the Great Kei further south, stretches the Wild Coast. This beautiful region was formerly part of the independent homeland of Transkei, but has now been incorporated into the Eastern Cape province. The sandy bays and rocky coves along this spectacular coast, although often difficult to access from the main road, are becoming increasingly popular. The scenery is breathtaking and the fishing along this coast is reputed to be excellent, from flimsy mackerel to shark weighing 450kg (990lb).

ACCOMMODATION

Wild Coast Sun and Casino ★★★★★, Mzamba, tel: (039) 305-9111, fax: 305-2778; glitz and glamour.
Trennery's Hotel, tel: (0471) 2-5344; beautifully situated on the Great Kei River, in Kentani district.

TRAVEL TIPS

The N2 bisects this region, passing north to south from Port Shepstone through Kokstad, Mount Frere, Umtata and Butterworth, where grocery supplies and petrol can be obtained. The gravel roads leading down to the coast can be rather taxing on both vehicle and driver. Beware of straying animals.

Above: *The strange detached cliff known as the Hole-in-the-Wall, is a well-known spot not far from Coffee Bay, on the beautiful Wild Coast.*

MAIN ATTRACTIONS

Wild Coast Sun: an extravagant, luxury hotel-casino complex situated right on the beachfront.
Hole-in-the-Wall: 1½ hours' walk south of Coffee Bay stands a massive, detached cliff with a small arched opening through which the surf thunders.
Mazeppa Bay: palm trees line three wide beaches; the scuba diving and snorkelling are good and the fishing is excellent.
Qora Mouth: a good beach with interesting rock pools, close to the hotel. The Dwesa and Cwebe nature reserves offer a combination of forest, grassland and rocky coastline that is populated by many birds and small mammals. Shell collecting is reputed to be very good here.
Fishing: fish caught along this coast range from kob, blacktail bronze bream and shad to barracuda and trophy-sized sharks.

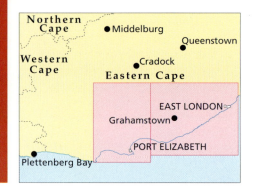

EASTERN CAPE

The Eastern Cape's shoreline extends from the KwaZulu-Natal border southwards to the Storms River mouth, incorporating the previously independent 'homelands' of Transkei and Ciskei. This beautiful region has an extremely turbulent history. It was here that 19th-century white settlers and black tribesmen fought bitterly for territorial possession, a confrontation that began in 1820 with the arrival in Algoa Bay of some 4000 British immigrants.

USEFUL CONTACTS

Eastern Cape Tourism Board,
Port Elizabeth, tel: (041) 55-7761.
Wild Coast region, tel: (0471) 31-2885.
Grahamstown Tourism,
tel: (0461) 2-3241, fax: 2-3266.
NSRI (Sea Rescue), tel: (041) 55-6011.
Computicket, tel: (041) 34-4550.
Accommodation Bureau,
tel: (041) 35-3248.

ACCOMMODATION

Fish River
Tsolwana Game Park and **Great Fish River Reserve**; for bookings at either reserve , tel: (0401) 95-2115, fax: 9-2756.
Hogsback
Hogsback Inn ★★, tel: (045) 962-1006, fax: 962-1015; surrounded by forest; beautiful nature walks and prolific birdlife.

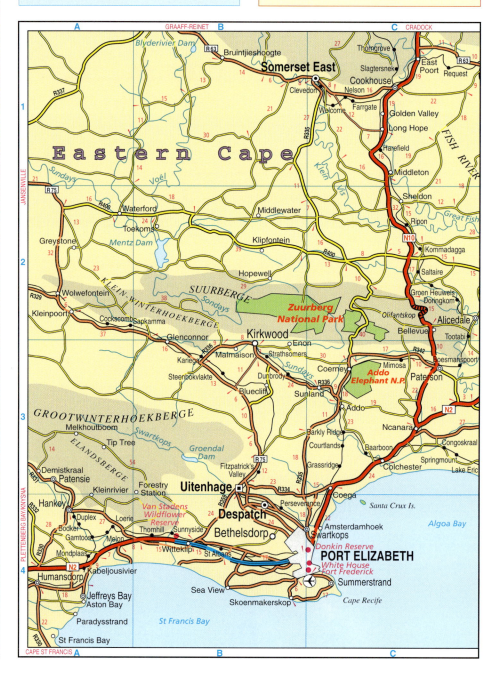

TRAVEL TIPS

The N2 leads west to Cape Town and northeast to Durban. The R32 links Port Elizabeth with Cradock. Wild Coast resorts are accessible via subsidiary (often gravel) roads leading off the N2. Beware of potholes, hairpin bends and straying animals.

P. E.	J	F	M	A	M	J	J	A	S	O	N	D
AV. TEMP. °C	21	21	20	18	16	14	14	14	15	17	18	20
AV. TEMP. °F	70	70	68	64	61	57	57	57	59	63	64	68
DAILY SUN hrs	9	8	7	7	7	7	7	8	7	8	9	7
RAINFALL mm	41	39	55	57	68	61	54	75	70	59	49	34
RAINFALL in	2	2	2.5	2.5	3	2.5	2.5	3	3	2.5	2	1.5
SEA TEMP. °C	21	21	20	19	17	16	16	16	17	18	19	21
SEA TEMP. °F	70	70	68	66	63	61	61	61	63	64	66	70

Right: *Every July Grahamstown swarms with visitors during the colourful National Arts Festival.*

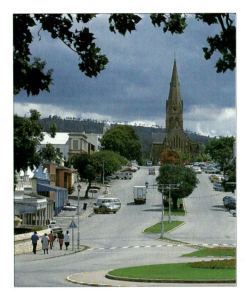

MAIN ATTRACTIONS

Jeffreys Bay: a surfer's paradise.
Grahamstown: academic and cultural centre; hosts acclaimed National Arts Festival each July.
Great Fish River Reserve: home to hippo, buffalo and black rhino.
Tsolwana Game Reserve: truly magnificent mountain reserve.
Hogsback: northwest of King William's Town, set among the exquisite forests which provided the inspiration for JRR Tolkien's novel, *The Hobbit*.
Port Alfred: pretty resort town at the mouth of the Kei River.

KEY TOURIST AREAS

PORT ELIZABETH

Known as the 'friendly city' and also as the 'windy city', Port Elizabeth is the economic hub of the Eastern Cape, much of its industrial activity revolving around the vehicle assembly sector and related concerns. P.E., as it is most often called, is also a major tourist centre. Set on the shores of Algoa Bay, the country's fifth-largest city has some excellent beaches, many historic buildings, sophisticated shopping centres, good hotels and restaurants. Port Elizabeth owes its origins to the 4000 British settlers who landed here in 1820.

MAIN ATTRACTIONS

Beaches: Port Elizabeth has four major beaches: King's, Humewood, Hobie and Pollok, each with its own special attractions.
Oceanarium and Museum Complex: at Humewood; see the performing dolphins and seals and visit the Aquarium and Snake Park.
Nature rambles: in and around P.E. lie **St George's Park** and the **Pearson Conservatory, Settler's Park**, the **Island Conservation Area** and the beautifully tended **Van Staden's Wildflower Reserve**.

Addo Elephant National Park: this park, located about 72km (45 miles) northeast of the city, was created in 1931 to protect the few remaining survivors of the once-prolific herds of Cape elephant. The sanctuary offers good game-viewing and comfortable accommodation.
Donkin Heritage Trail: a steeply winding historical walking tour.
Fort Frederick: building of historical significance built in 1799; located on Belmont Terrace, overlooking the Baakens River estuary.

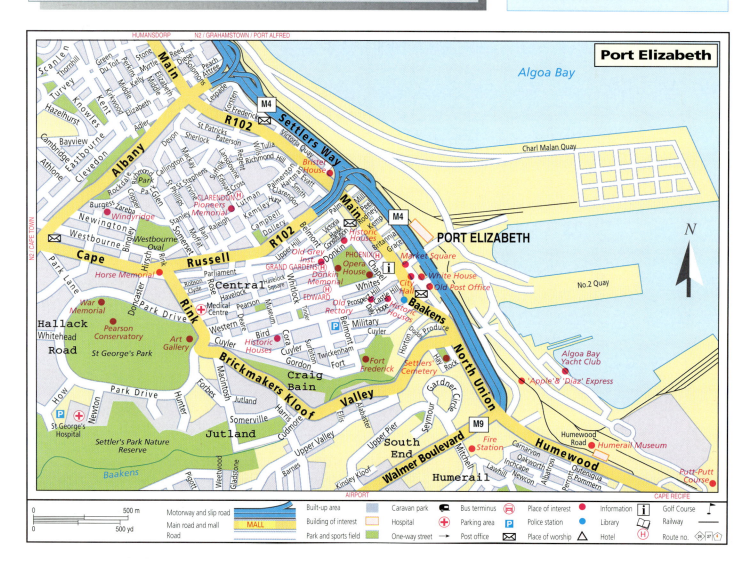

EAST LONDON

Situated at the mouth of the Buffalo River, the river port of East London combines the charm of a relatively small community with all the essential amenities of a large city. Its attractions are of the quiet, undemanding, family-orientated kind: it has fine beaches, pleasant parks and gardens, good hotels and restaurants, and some entertaining nightlife in the summer months, especially in the seafront area. The principal thoroughfare, Oxford Street, is lined with a variety of modern shops, many of which cater to the tourist trade. The port serves the industries of the Eastern Cape and the Free State.

ACCOMMODATION

Holiday Inn Garden Court East London ★★★, cnr. John Bailey and Moore Streets, tel: (0431) 2-7260, fax: 43-7360; on beachfront.
Kennaway Hotel ★★★, tel: (0431) 2-5531, fax: 2-5531; close to the city centre and the beaches.
Esplanade Hotel ★★, tel: (0431) 2-2518, fax: 2-3679; conveniently situated on the main beachfront.

Kidds Beach Hotel, Main Road, Kidds Beach, tel: (0432) 81-1715, fax: 81-1852; country hotel five minutes from the beachfront.
Blue Lagoon Hotel, Blue Bend Place, Beacon Bay, tel: (0431) 47-4821, fax: 47-2037; very close to the beach.
The Hornbills, 28 Lotus Avenue, Bonza Bay, tel/fax: (0431) 47-1789; bed and breakfast establishment.

MAIN ATTRACTIONS

Superb beaches: most popular and accessible is Orient Beach.
East London Museum: Oxford Street; exhibits include the first coelacanth (a species of fish hitherto considered extinct) and the world's only dodo egg.
Aquarium: over 400 species.
Queen's Park Botanical Gardens: splendour of indigenous flora.
Ann Bryant Gallery: fine local paintings and sculptures.
Hiking trails: a choice of walks from the 4-day Shipwreck Trail to the 2-hour Umtiza Trail lead nature lovers along unspoilt beaches, through nature reserves, or into the Amatola mountains to the northwest of East London.

KEY TOURIST AREAS

East London

	Built-up area	Caravan park	Bus terminus	Place of interest	Information	Golf Course

0   250 m
0   250 yd
Motorway and slip road · Main road and mall · Road
Built-up area · Building of interest · Park and sports field
Caravan park · Hospital · One-way street
Bus terminus · Parking area · Post office
Place of interest · Police station · Place of worship
Information · Library · Hotel
Golf Course · Railway · Route no.

GARDEN ROUTE

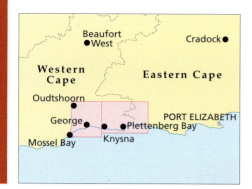

The Western Cape coastal terrace, extending from the Storms River and the Tsitsikamma area in the east to Mossel Bay in the west, is known as the Garden Route. This is an enchanting shoreline of lovely bays and coves, high cliffs and wide estuaries, with a hinterland of mountains, spectacular passes, rivers, waterfalls and wooded ravines. The lagoons and lakes around Knysna and Wilderness are magical stretches of water. The attractions are many: good hotels and eating places, pleasant villages and resorts, and a warm ocean that beckons bather, yachtsman and angler alike. Further inland are the town of Oudtshoorn and its surrounding ostrich farms, as well as the magnificent Cango Caves.

ACCOMMODATION

Wilderness
Karos Wilderness Hotel ★★★★, tel: (044) 877-1110, fax: 887-1910; surrounded by unspoilt nature; heated pools.
Fairy Knowe Hotel ★★, tel: (044) 877-1100, fax: 877-0364; on the banks of the Touw River.
Baywater Village, tel: (04455) 3-2008, fax: 3-2688; serviced chalets.

Knysna
Brenton-on-Sea Hotel ★★★, tel: (0445) 81-0081, fax: 81-0026; 15km (9 miles) from Knysna.
Plettenberg Bay
Beacon Island Hotel ★★★, tel: (04457) 3-1120, fax: 3-3880; smart hotel in a unique setting.
Formosa Bay Hotel, tel: (04457) 3-2060, fax: 3-3343; estate on N2.

Stromboli's Inn ★★★, tel: (04457) 7710, fax: 7823; between Wilderness and Tsitsikamma.
Sedgefield
Lake Pleasant Hotel ★★★, tel: (04455) 3-1313, fax: 3-2040; bass lake.
Oudtshoorn
Riempie Estate Hotel ★★★, tel: (0443) 22-6161, fax: 22-6772; close to Highgate Ostrich Farm.

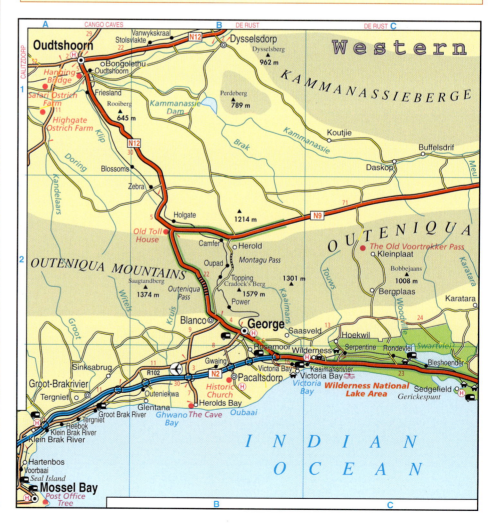

MOSSEL BAY	J	F	M	A	M	J	J	A	S	O	N	D
AV. TEMP. °C	21	21	20	18	17	16	15	15	16	17	18	20
AV. TEMP. °F	70	70	68	64	63	61	59	59	61	63	64	68
DAILY SUN hrs	7	7	7	7	7	7	7	7	7	7	7	7
RAINFALL mm	28	31	36	40	37	31	32	36	39	38	34	28
RAINFALL in	1	1	1.5	2	1.5	1	1	1.5	2	1.5	1.5	1
SEA TEMP. °C	22	22	20	19	18	16	16	16	16	17	19	21
SEA TEMP. °F	72	72	68	66	64	61	61	61	61	63	66	70

MAIN ATTRACTIONS

Tsitsikamma National Park and **Otter Trail:** an 80km (50-mile) strip of superb coastline and large offshore marine reserve.
Storms River Mouth: dramatic scenery at this spectacular site; spend a night in the chalets.
Plettenberg Bay: fashionable holiday resort with beautiful beaches.
Mossel Bay: excellent beaches and the Bartolomeu Dias Museum.
Goukamma Nature Reserve: short distance west of Knysna; unspoilt nature and wonderful birdlife.

Garden of Eden: a beautiful forest area; many of its trees are labelled.
Knysna: charming little resort town with an attractive lagoon.
Wilderness Lake Area: superb scenery and prolific birdlife.
Oudtshoorn: famous for its fascinating ostrich farms.
Cango Caves: complex of caverns ranked among the most remarkable of Africa's many natural wonders.
Bungi jumping: only the brave will attempt the awesome jump off Gourits River bridge.

DISTANCE IN KM FROM GEORGE	
Bloemfontein	773
Cape Town	438
Durban	1319
Johannesburg	1171
Port Elizabeth	335

Left: *The Tsitsikamma Trail offers hikers an opportunity to enjoy the serene countryside.*

USEFUL CONTACTS

Tsitsikamma National Park, tel: (042) 541-1607, fax: 541-1629.
Oudtshoorn Publicity Association, tel: (0443) 22-2228.
Mossel Bay Marketing Association, tel: (0444) 91-2202.
Plettenberg Bay Info, tel: (04457) 3-4065.

Map

WILLOWMORE

Cape

Eastern

KOUGABERGE

Cape

Mannetjiesberg ▲ 1955 m

Zaaimansdal

Sipres

Smutsberg ▲ 1757m

Uniondale · Historic Fort & Watermill

Potjiesberg Pass

Hoopsberg ▲ 1706m

Uniondale Poort ▲ 1155 m

DIE LANGKLOOF

Dwaas

Skrik

Kouga

N9 R62

Avontuur Siesta Haarlem

Lutheran Mission Church

Gaviota

Ongelegen

Misgund

Nuweplaas

Bruinklip

Louterwater

Krakeelrivier

Noll

1320m

Prince Alfreds Pass

De Vlug

LANGKLOOFBERGE

Krakeelrivier

Joubertina

Tweeriviere

MOUNTAINS

Klein-Palmiet

Dwars

Palmiet

Thumb Peak ▲ 1424m

▲ Peak Formosa 1675m

TSITSIKAMMABERGE

Kruisvallei

Keurbooms

Whiskey Creek Nature Reserve

Groot

Bloukrans

Grenadier's Cap ▲ 987m

Tsitsikamma Forest Reserve

Stormsrivier ▲ 1680m

Barrington

Homtini Pass

Rooiels

Goukamma

Steenbras

Prince Alfreds Pass

R340

Keurbooms River Nature Reserve

Bietou

Viewpoint

The Crags

Bloukrans Pass

Coldstream

Grootrivier Pass

Nature's Valley

Paul Sauer Bridge

HUMANSDORP

Die Hoek

Knysna

Phantom Pass

Knysna National Lake Area

The Big Tree

Keurboomstrand

N2

Stormsrivier

Tsitsikamma National Park

Supension Bridge

Ruigtevlei Mielierug

N2

Keytersnek

Knysna

R339

Wittedrif

N2

Keurboomsrivier

Dolphin Viewpoint

Groenvlei

Goukamma Nature Reserve

Brenton

Hornlee

Noetzie

Plettenberg Bay

Brenton-on-Sea

Buffelsbaai

Walker Point

East Cape

The Heads

Walker Bay

Legend

0 — 15 km	National road & motorway N4	Distances	Highland
0 — 15 miles	Principal road	Scenic route	National park
	Main road	Mountain pass	Water feature
	Minor road	Interchange	Place of interest ●

Hotel (H)	City	Small town ○
Railway station ●	Camp ⌂	Major town ■
Camp	Large village ◎
Peak in metres ▲	Toll road (T)	Town
Place of interest ●	Town	Village ○

GEORGE

This pleasant little town, which was named after England's King George III, has some 75,000 inhabitants, lies at the foot of the Outeniqua Mountains and is the Garden Route's principal urban centre. The surrounding countryside is devoted to general farming, forestry and the cultivation of hops. The town is linked to Knysna by the main Garden Route highway. George is also the aerial gateway to the region.

Above: *The Van Kervel Gardens near George — a tranquil haven of lush vegetation, still waters and rich birdlife, overlooked by the Outeniqua range.*

USEFUL CONTACTS

George Information Bureau, 124 York Street, tel: (044) 863-9295, fax: 73-5228; tourist information and advice.

MAIN ATTRACTIONS

Outeniqua Choo-Tjoe: this old steam train will take you on a scenic day trip to Knysna.
George Museum: in the Old Drostdy; noted for its antique musical instruments.
Churches: visit St Mark's, South Africa's smallest cathedral; the Dutch Reformed church, completed in 1842, has a fine hardwood interior; and St Peter and St Paul is the oldest Roman Catholic church in the country.
Beaches: excellent bathing, fishing and sun-worshipping at Herold's and Victoria bays.

ACCOMMODATION

Fancourt Hotel ★★★★★, tel: (044) 70-8282, fax: 70-7605; elegant, with excellent golfing facilities.
Far Hills Protea Hotel ★★★, tel: (044) 71-1295, fax: 71-1951; over-looks the Outeniqua mountains.
Hoogekraal Country House, tel: (044) 79-1277, fax: 79-1300; well-kept 18th-century homestead; SATOUR-acclaimed.

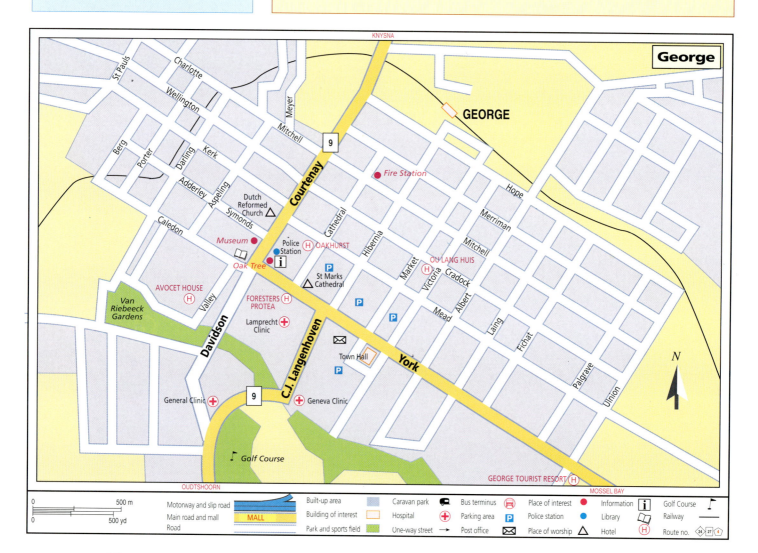

KNYSNA

Knysna is celebrated for its locally brewed draught ale (Mitchell's), its fresh oysters, and the fine furniture made from the area's hardwoods. The biggest drawcard, however, is Knysna Lagoon: a stretch of water guarded by two sandstone cliffs known as The Heads. The lagoon, popular with boating enthusiasts, waterskiers and anglers, harbours a variety of fish and water-birds, 'pansy shells' and a rare species of sea horse. Cabin cruisers and houseboats may be hired; the John Benn, a 20-ton pleasure boat, leaves from the jetty each morning (sightseeing, live entertainment, wining and dining on board).

USEFUL CONTACTS

Knysna Hospital, tel: (0445) 2-3123.
Knysna Tourism, tel: (0445) 82-5510.
Featherbed Bay Nature Reserve, tel: (0445) 2-1693; free ferry ride across the bay to the lovely reserve, where you can hike, picnic or dine in style at the restaurant.

KNYSNA	J	F	M	A	M	J	J	A	S	O	N	D
AV. TEMP. °C	21	21	20	18	17	16	15	15	16	17	18	20
AV. TEMP. °F	70	70	68	64	63	61	59	59	61	63	64	68
DAILY SUN hrs	7	7	7	7	7	7	7	7	7	7	7	7
RAINFALL mm	28	31	36	40	37	31	32	36	39	38	34	28
RAINFALL in	1	1	1.5	2	1.5	1	1	1.5	2	1.5	1.5	1
SEA TEMP. °C	22	22	20	19	18	16	16	16	16	17	19	21
SEA TEMP. °F	72	72	68	66	64	61	61	61	61	63	66	70

ACCOMMODATION

Old Drift Forest Lodges ★★★, tel/fax: (0445) 2-1994; comfortable, self-catering log chalets in a beautiful forest setting; a paradise for birdwatchers.
Belvidere Manor, tel: (0445) 387-1055, fax: 387-1059; historic home at the edge of the lagoon; dates back to 1834.
Under Milk Wood, tel: (0445) 2-2385, fax: 2-2494; self-catering holiday log cabins situated right on lovely Knysna Lagoon.
Overlander's Lodge, tel: (0445) 82-5920; convenient, affordable backpackers' accommodation.

MAIN ATTRACTIONS

Knysna Heads: two imposing promontories which guard the entrance to Knysna Lagoon and provide good views of the surrounding area.
Royal Hotel: Prince Alfred and George Bernard Shaw stayed here.
Millwood Museum: local history, gold mining and timber industry.
Fresh oysters: try some, sprinkled with fresh lemon juice or hot chilli sauce, at the Knysna Oyster Co.
Crab's Creek: a restaurant on the water's edge; sit under umbrellas and enjoy the prolific birdlife.
Noetzie: stroll past the five castles on the sea (please note that they are private residences).
Knysna Forest: together with the Tsitsikamma Forest, forms the largest expanse of indigenous high forest in South Africa.
Die Ou Fabriek: arts and crafts on offer in the garden of Craft House.

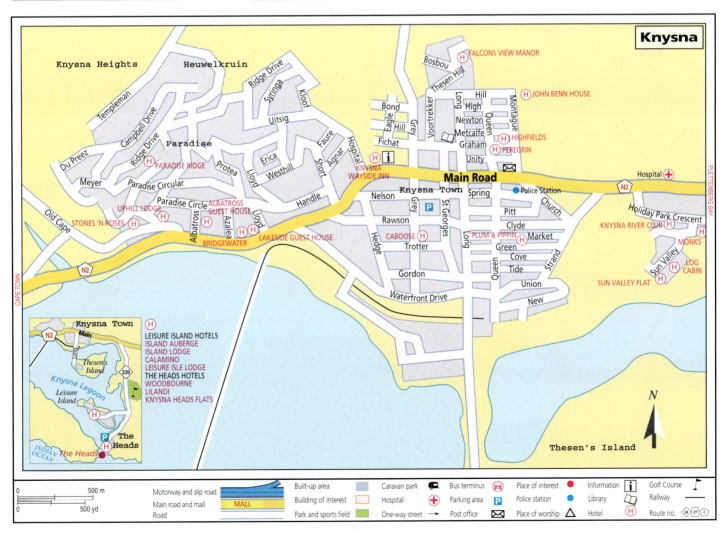

CAPE WINELANDS

*W*ithin easy reach of Cape Town lie a number of superb vineyards, some of which have achieved international acclaim. Begin your tour in elegant Constantia, on the eastern slopes of the mountain, with its four choice estates. But quaint country towns such as Stellenbosch, Paarl, Grabouw, Franschhoek and Somerset West, with their stately Cape-Dutch homes, form the hub of South Africa's wine-making industry.

MAIN ATTRACTIONS

Stellenbosch: hub of the wineland region; a picturesque town that prides itself on its lovely historic buildings and oak-lined avenues.

Franschhoek: founded by French Huguenots between 1680 and 1690. Protestant settlers were forbidden to form independent communities and, through intermarriage, lost much of their cultural heritage, but they left an indelible mark on the local wine-growing industry.

Paarl: original farming settlement established in 1720; visit a number of splendid wine estates in the vicinity of this little town.

Somerset West: the beautiful big homestead of Vergelegen estate was built by an early Cape governor and completed in 1701.

Right: *The wide and fertile Hex River Valley supports some 200 farms. By late autumn the surrounding mountains are often dusted with snow.*

DISTANCE IN KM FROM CAPE TOWN	
Constantia	10
Franschhoek	57
Paarl	58
Stellenbosch	42

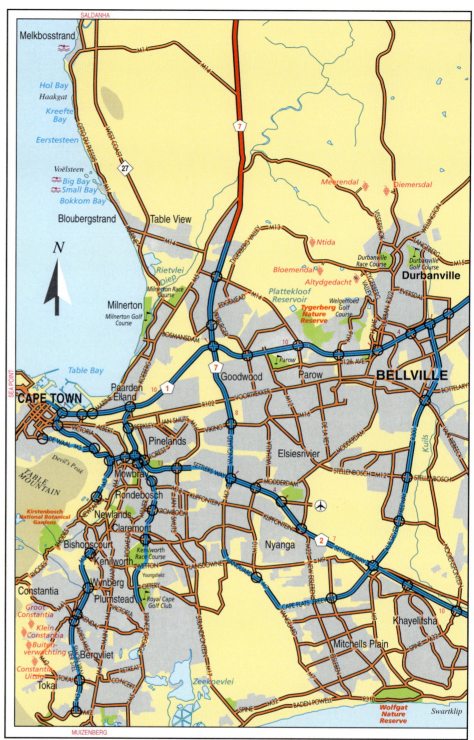

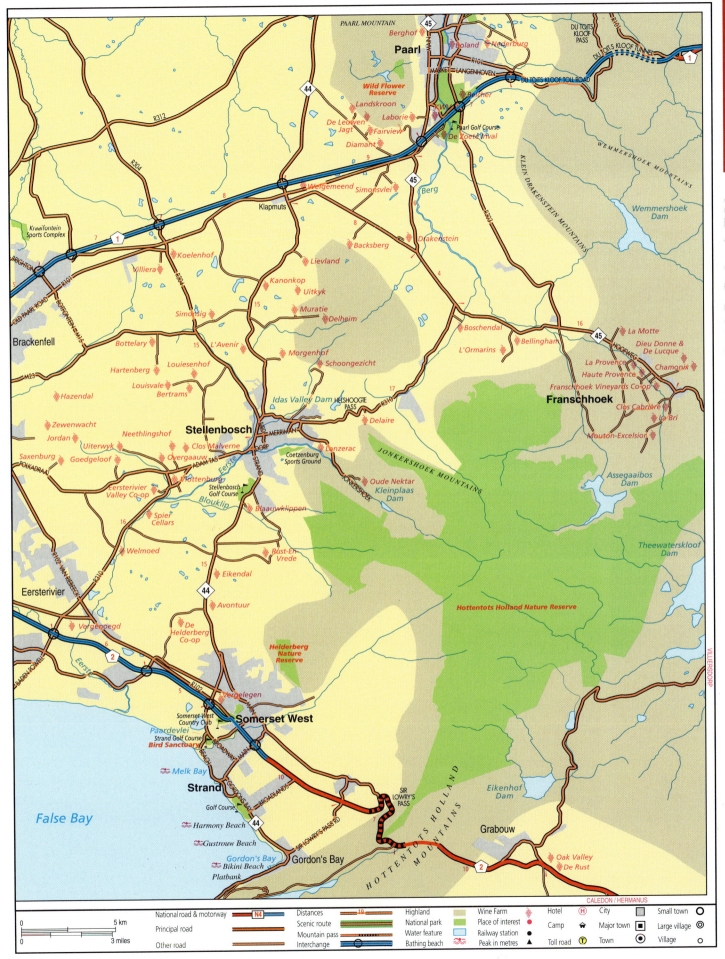

KEY TOURIST AREAS

National road & motorway	N4	
Principal road		
Other road		
Distances		
Scenic route		
Mountain pass		
Interchange		
Highland		
National park		
Water feature		
Railway station		
Bathing beach		
Wine Farm		Hotel	H City
Place of interest		Camp	Major town
Peak in metres		Toll road	T Town
			Small town
			Large village
			Village

0 — 5 km
0 — 3 miles

STELLENBOSCH AND PAARL

Charming Stellenbosch, less than an hour's drive from Cape Town, lies in the Eerste River Valley. The town is very proud of its heritage – a fact that is evident in the original watering system, old churchyards and well-maintained gabled buildings along the oak-lined streets. Stellenbosch is a leading centre of learning; university and town integrate harmoniously. Paarl, the biggest of the wineland towns, began as a farming and wagon-building settlement in 1720 and was named after the granite rock that resembles a giant pearl on the overlooking mountain. Both the mountain and its surrounds are maintained as a nature reserve; there's a circular route to the top.

ACCOMMODATION

Grande Roche Hotel ★★★★★, tel: (021) 863-2727, fax: 863-2220; elegant hotel with award-winning Bosman's Restaurant.
Lanzerac Manor and Winery ★★★★, tel: (021) 887-1132, fax: 887-2310; superb facilities, elegantly refurbished; wine made on the premises.
D'Ouwe Werf ★★★, tel: (021) 887-4608, fax: 887-4626; tradition and atmosphere combined.
Roggeland Country House, tel: (021) 868-2501, fax: 868-2113; internationally acclaimed.

USEFUL CONTACTS

Stellenbosch Hospital, tel: (021) 887-0310.
Stellenbosch Wine Route, tel: (021) 886-4310.
Stellenbosch Information Office, tel: (021) 883-9633.

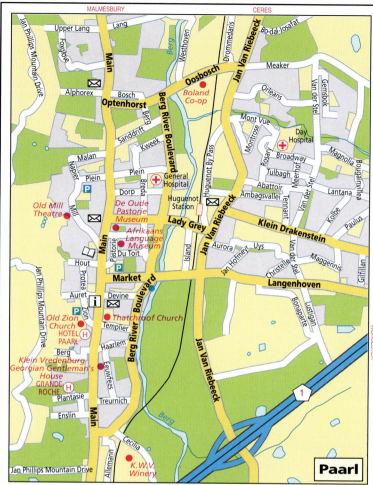

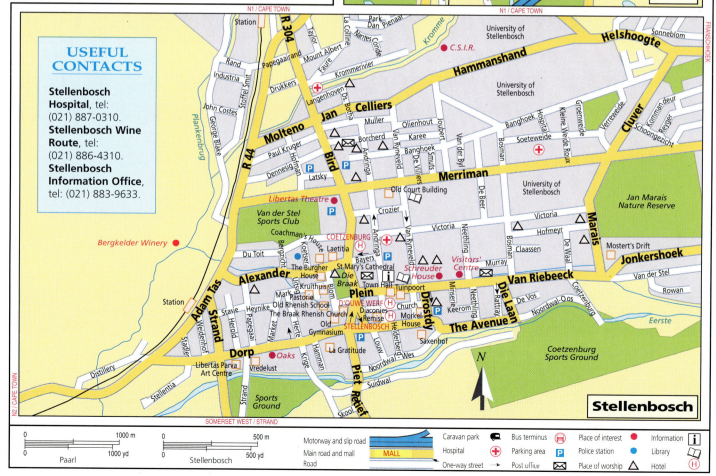

WEST COAST

*T*he harsh western shores of the country, pounded by the icy Atlantic Ocean, are a rather barren region of low coastal vegetation. Sleepy fishing villages bake in the sun, while further inland little farming communities huddle together in the wide, vast emptiness. But the area is transformed after the spring rains, when a carpet of flowers erupts in a riot of colour stretching as far as the eye can see.

MAIN ATTRACTIONS

Langebaan Lagoon: a sweeping lagoon bordered by an unspoilt beach dotted with little holiday cottages. **Club Mykonos** nearby is a resort hotel for those who like to holiday in style.

West Coast National Park: beautiful natural wetland reserve with prolific **birdlife** and magnificent wildflowers each spring (August–October). The **Flowerline** provides useful information about the best displays, tel: (021) 418-3705.

Elandsbaai: buy some crayfish fresh from the factory.

Above: *After the spring rains, the parched land lies resplendent in a colourful tapestry of flowers.*

ACCOMMODATION

Protea Saldanha Bay ★★★, 51 Main Street, Saldanha, tel: (02281) 4-1264, fax: 4-4093.

Marine Protea Hotel ★★★, Lambert's Bay, tel: (027) 432-1126, fax: 432-1036; a comfortable and friendly establishment.

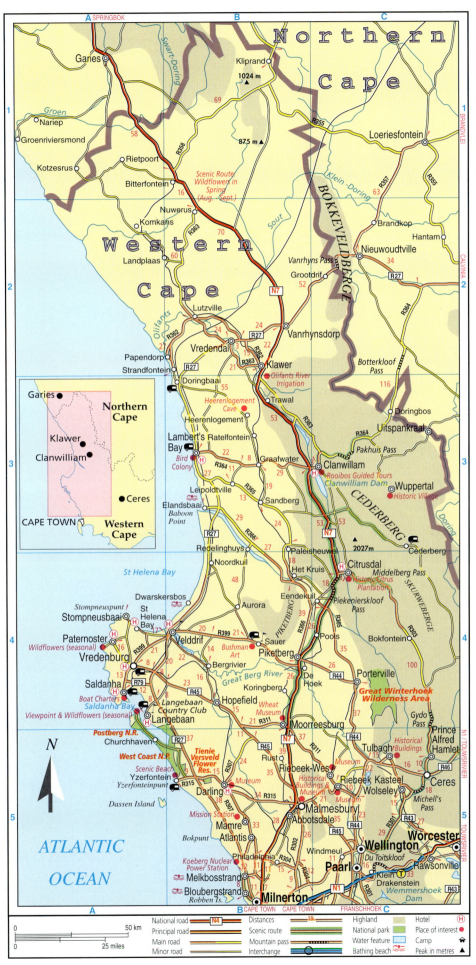

CAPE PENINSULA

*T*he Cape Peninsula stretches from the Cape of Good Hope and Cape Point northward to Table Bay and comprises, for the most part, a strikingly beautiful plateau that achieves its loftiest and most spectacular heights in the famed Table Mountain massif overlooking Table Bay and Cape Town — a neat bustling little metropolis of handsome buildings, elegant thoroughfares and glittering shops. The western and eastern shorelines of the Peninsula are graced by superb beaches and attractive residential and resort centres that are a magnet for holiday-makers, scuba divers, boating enthusiasts, surfers and sun-worshippers.

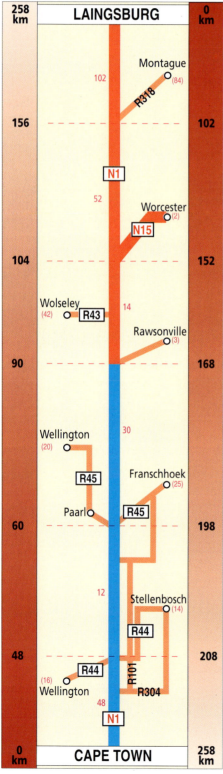

ACCOMMODATION

Lord Charles Hotel ★★★★, Somerset West, tel: (021) 855-1040, fax: 855-1107; gracious elegance; world-class.
Karos Arthur's Seat Hotel ★★★★, Sea Point, tel: (021) 434-1187, fax: 434-9768; stylish accommodation.
Alphen Hotel ★★★★, tel: (021) 794-5011, fax: 794-5710; charming wine estate in Constantia Valley.
Peninsula All-Suite Hotel ★★★★, Sea Point, tel: (021) 439-8888, fax: 439-8886; on the promenade.
Holiday Inn Garden Court Newlands ★★★, tel: (021) 61-1105, fax: 64-1241; close to the cricket ground and rugby stadium.
The Lord Nelson Inn ★★★, Simon's Town, tel: (021) 786-1386, fax: 786-1009; colonial-style inn offering old-fashioned hospitality.
Shrimpton Manor ★★, Muizenberg, tel: (021) 788-5225, fax: 788-1120; whale-watching from the rooftop.
The Adams Family Guest House, Muizenberg, tel: (021) 788-9156, fax: 788-9157; overlooks False Bay.

TRAVEL TIPS

Rail, bus and taxi services are adequate. Major international car-hire companies are represented, as are local car, camper, and caravan-hire firms. Tour operators offer a wide choice of one-day and half-day scenic coach trips.
Please note: South African taxis must be booked or boarded at the designated stands, as they do not cruise for fares.

Above: *A funicular railway takes visitors up to the lookout at Cape Point for panoramic views of False Bay and the southern Atlantic Ocean.*

MAIN ATTRACTIONS

Cape Town: this charming metropolis, overshadowed by its Table Mountain, is the country's oldest urban centre.
Table Mountain: ride the cableway or climb up to the summit and marvel at the spectacular views.
Kirstenbosch: one of the world's most celebrated botanical gardens.
The V&A Waterfront: at the docks; a sophisticated complex of restaurants, shops and pubs.
Sea Point: a busy cosmopolitan seaside suburb with numerous good restaurants.
Clifton: chic suburb noted for its four magnificent beaches; popular with the trendier set.

Chapman's Peak Drive: a world-famous drive with dramatic views of the surf 600m (1980ft) below, at the foot of a sheer drop.
Hout Bay: enchanting little suburb with a quaint fishing harbour.
Cape Point: southernmost tip of the peninsula; the finest of view sites.
Simon's Town: the headquarters of the South African Navy, noted for its old-world charm and proximity to the fine beaches of Seaforth, as well as the jackass penguin colony at Boulders.
Constantia Wine Estates: four estates in the beautiful Constantia Valley: Groot and Klein Constantia, Buitenverwachting and Uitsig.

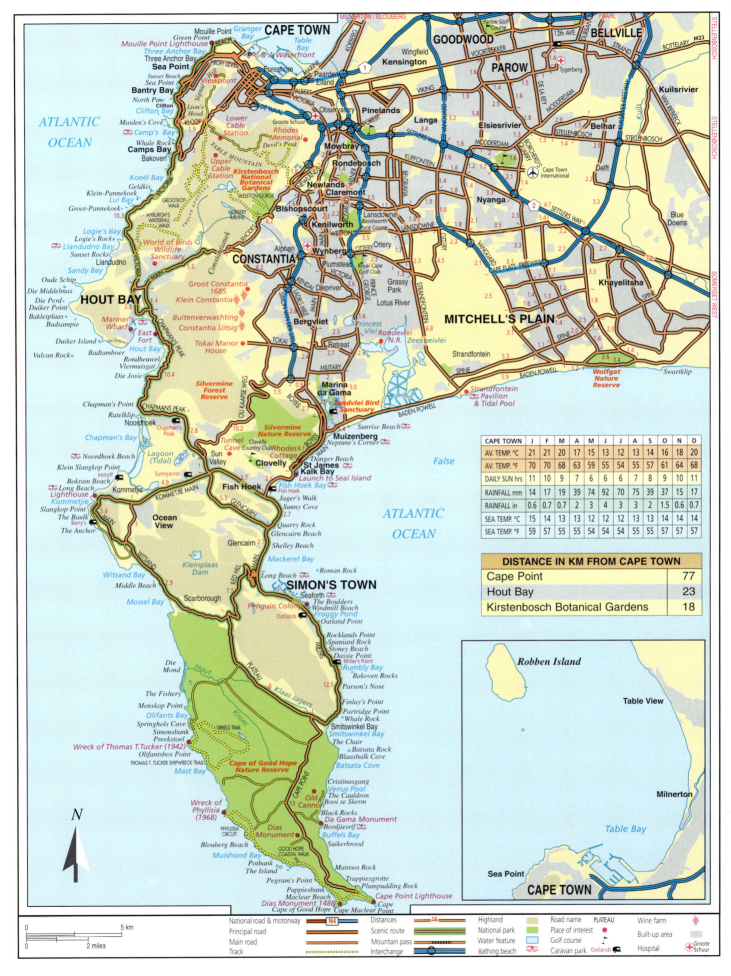

KEY TOURIST AREAS

CAPE TOWN	J	F	M	A	M	J	J	A	S	O	N	D
AV. TEMP. °C	21	21	20	17	15	13	12	13	14	16	18	20
AV. TEMP. °F	70	70	68	63	59	55	54	55	57	61	64	68
DAILY SUN hrs	11	10	9	7	6	6	6	7	8	9	10	11
RAINFALL mm	14	17	19	39	74	92	70	75	39	37	15	17
RAINFALL in	0.6	0.7	0.7	2	3	4	3	3	2	1.5	0.6	0.7
SEA TEMP. °C	15	14	13	13	12	12	12	13	13	14	14	14
SEA TEMP. °F	59	57	55	55	54	54	54	55	55	57	57	57

DISTANCE IN KM FROM CAPE TOWN	
Cape Point	77
Hout Bay	23
Kirstenbosch Botanical Gardens	18

47

KIRSTENBOSCH

*T*he Kirstenbosch National Botanical Garden lies on the eastern slopes of the Table Mountain range. An astonishing array of flowering plants, representative of about a quarter of South Africa's 24,000 species, are cultivated here. Delightful walks lead through herb and fragrance gardens, and through stinkwood and yellow-wood groves. There is a pelargonium koppie and a cycad amphitheatre, and the birdlife, particularly the sunbirds drawn to the collection of protaceae, is enchanting.

ENCHANTED GARDEN

Braille walk/perfume garden: designed especially for blind visitors.
Restaurant: for a relaxing stop; overlooking the gardens.
Jan van Riebeeck's hedge: part of the original wild almond hedge planted by the first Dutch settlers.
Compton Herbarium: contains over 200,000 plant specimens.
Sunday concerts: spend an enchanted summer evening listening to music and picnicking, while the setting sun illuminates the magnificent mountain, creating a superb backdrop.

Left: *The rugged east face of the Table Mountain massif frames the delicate beauty of Kirstenbosch.*

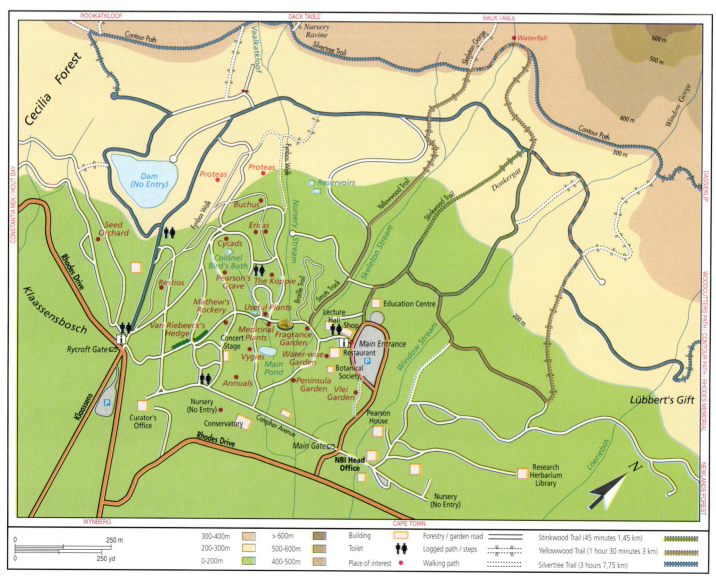

CAPE TOWN

The central metropolitan area of Cape Town huddles in a 'bowl' formed by the majestic Table Mountain, its flanking peaks and the broad sweep of Table Bay. Founded by Dutch settlers in 1652, Cape Town is the country's oldest city and fourth largest in terms of population. More than 300 years of history have created its unique character – a vibrant blend of Dutch, French, English and Malay influences. It is an attractive, colourful city that boasts excellent hotels and restaurants, open-air markets and shops catering for every pocket and taste. Fortunately for visitors, the compactness of central Cape Town makes it ideal for exploring on foot.

MAIN ATTRACTIONS

Table Mountain: ride the revamped cable car or hike to the summit, and enjoy the breathtaking views.

Castle of Good Hope: the city's most notable landmark (built between 1666 and 1679).

Victoria and Alfred Waterfront: complex of shops, restaurants and pubs in a working harbour.

Two Oceans Aquarium: at the Waterfront; unique underwater experience of kelp forests, touch pools and gigantic aquariums.

St George's Cathedral: see the famous Rose Window in this lovely church and have tea in the crypt.

Greenmarket Square: for bargain hunting in one of Africa's prettiest little plazas. Be sure not to miss the **Old Town House** (built 1761) which contains the Michaelis collection of 17-century Dutch and Flemish art.

The Company Gardens: take a walk through the lush gardens originally founded by Jan Van Riebeeck to supply fresh fruit and vegetables to the Dutch East India Company ships. While here, visit the South African Museum, the Planetarium, and the National Art Gallery.

Koopmans–De Wet House: admire the beautiful antique yellow- and stinkwood furniture.

Shopping: Cape Town's informal markets are the place to shop for contemporary African art, curios, ethnic jewellery and more. Try St George's Mall, Greenmarket Square and the Kirstenbosch Craft Market.

Rhodes Memorial: a grand monument with breathtaking views, located on the eastern slopes of Devil's Peak.

Signal Hill: have a sundowner and enjoy the panoramic view.

Bo-Kaap Museum: dedicated to the Malay culture; in one of the oldest original buildings.

Below: *To Capetonians, the arrival of the strong Southeaster gusts is heralded by the appearance of the famous 'tablecloth' over Table Mountain.*

Events and Festivals

Minstrel (Coon) Carnival: vibrant part of the **New Year** celebrations.

Metropolitan Handicap: exciting horseracing event held in **January**.

Spring Wildflower Show: held at Kirstenbosch in **September**.

Rothman's Sailing Week: colourful international regatta in **December**.

Two Oceans Marathon: this popular event takes place on **Easter Sunday**.

USEFUL CONTACTS

Groote Schuur Hospital, tel: (021) 404-9111.

Captour, tel: (021) 418-5214.

Computicket, tel: (021) 430-8080.

Table Mountain Aerial Cableway Co Ltd, tel: (021) 24-5148; information regarding weather conditions and visibility.

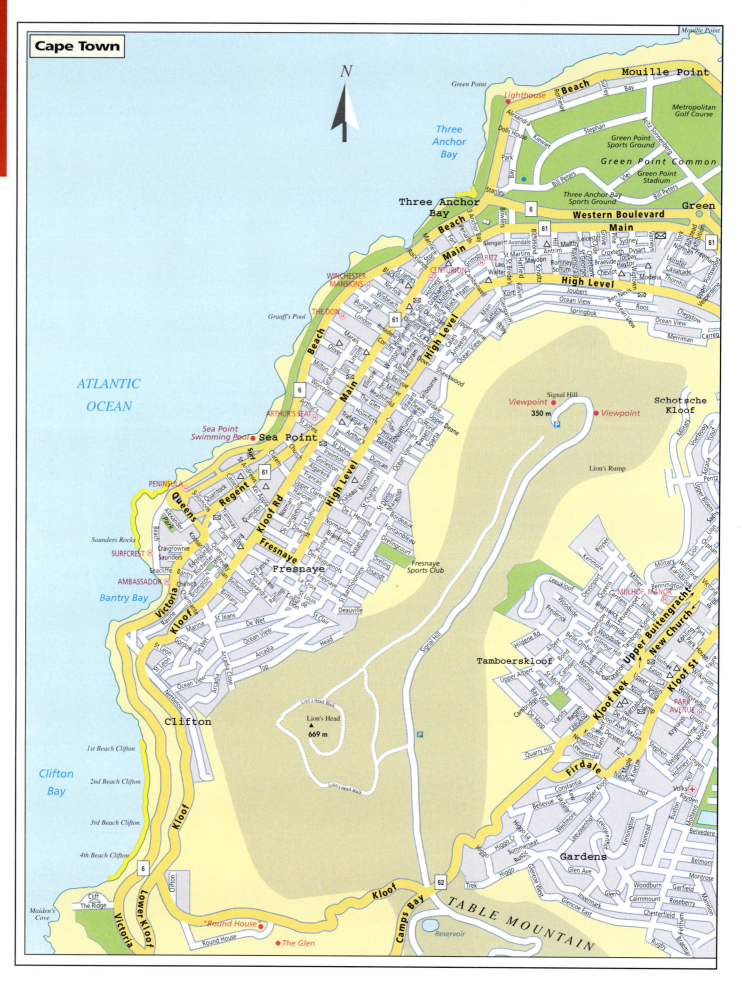

Cape Town

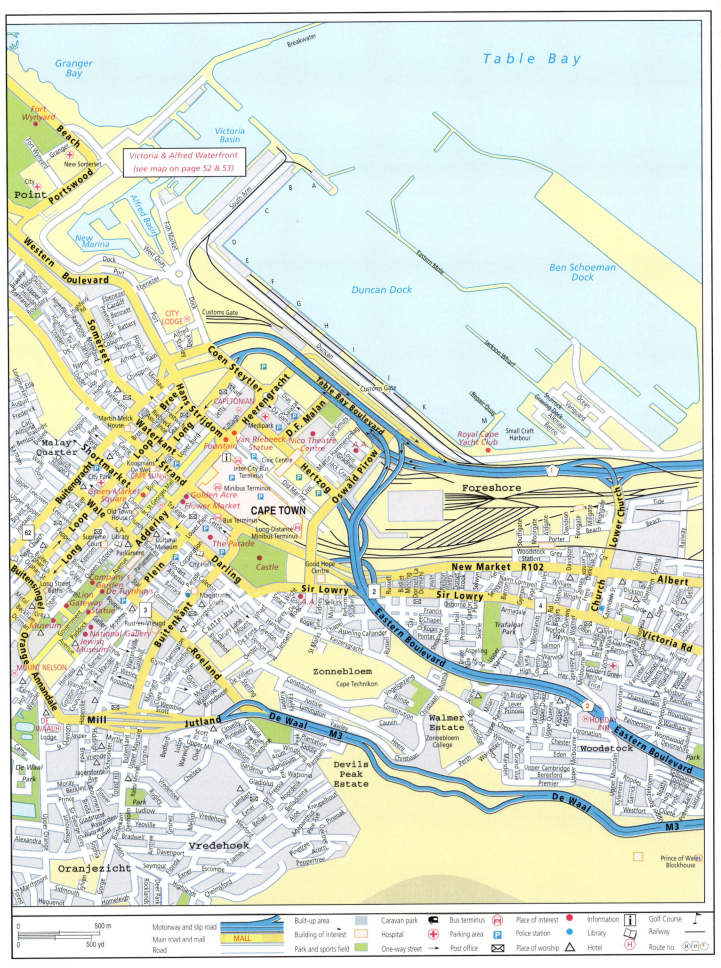

KEY TOURIST AREAS

Victoria & Alfred Waterfront
(see map on page 52 & 53)

V & A WATERFRONT

After a long separation, city and harbour are once again happily reunited through the ambitious Victoria and Alfred Waterfront redevelopment scheme, a multibillion-rand private venture that borrowed ideas from the successful harbour projects of New York, Vancouver and Sydney among others, yet retains a sparkling, lively character of its own.

ACCOMMODATION

The Table Bay Hotel ★★★★★, tel: (021) 406-5000, fax: 406-5686; elegant luxury; modern convenience.
Cape Grace Hotel ★★★★★, tel: (021) 410-7100, fax: 419-7622; on the West Quay, spectacular views.
Victoria and Alfred Hotel ★★★★, tel: (021) 419-6677, fax: 419-8955; alongside the Alfred Basin.
Victoria Junction Hotel ★★★★, Ebeneezer Road, Greenpoint, tel: (021) 418-1234, fax: 418-5678; avant-garde; loft-style Art Deco.
City Lodge Waterfront ★★, tel: (021) 419-9450, fax: 419-0460; convenient location at main entrance to the Waterfront.

MAIN ATTRACTIONS

Two Oceans Aquarium: an imaginative 35 million-rand complex of world-class standard; watch shoals of fish swim through giant aquariums and explore the touch pools.
South African Maritime Museum: on 4000m² (13,123ft²); the largest display of model ships in South Africa. There is also a discovery cove for the children.
SAS *Somerset*: explore this interesting floating exhibit.
Art and Craft Market: filled with an enormous variety of goods that will appeal to both young and old.
Telkom Exploratorium: hands-on look at the wonders of technology.
Imax: Five-storey cinema screen and high-tech surround-sound system at the BMW Pavilion.
The *Victoria*: a floating treasure museum that exhibits artefacts salvaged from ships wrecked along the coast of the Cape of Storms.
The King's Warehouse: sample the fare of the many diverse food stalls and shop at the huge fish market.
The Red Shed: watch artists at work as they create a variety of items, from delicate glass-blown flowers to colourful ethnic oil paintings and wooden toys.
Cape fur seals: a thriving, wild community of these mammals frequents the calm harbour waters. Watch them diving, lazily floating around, or basking in the sun.
Boat trips: a number of boats and smaller vessels are available for harbour and sunset cruises, as well as longer trips to historic **Robben Island**, the former prison enclave whose most famous inmate was President Nelson Mandela.

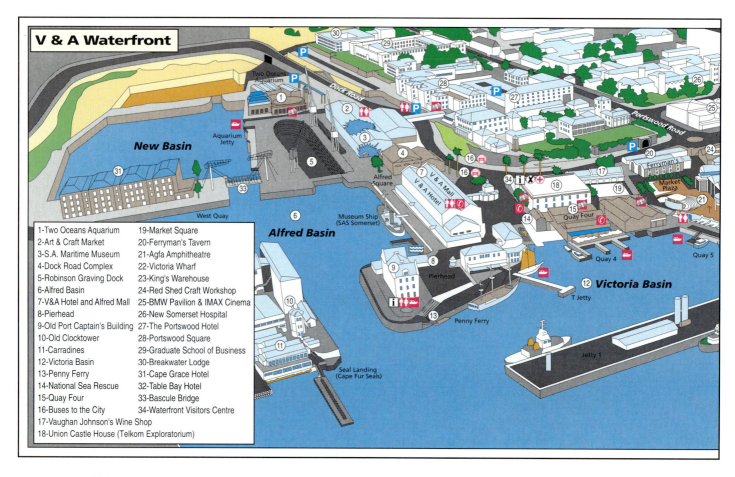

V & A Waterfront

1-Two Oceans Aquarium
2-Art & Craft Market
3-S.A. Maritime Museum
4-Dock Road Complex
5-Robinson Graving Dock
6-Alfred Basin
7-V&A Hotel and Alfred Mall
8-Pierhead
9-Old Port Captain's Building
10-Old Clocktower
11-Carradines
12-Victoria Basin
13-Penny Ferry
14-National Sea Rescue
15-Quay Four
16-Buses to the City
17-Vaughan Johnson's Wine Shop
18-Union Castle House (Telkom Exploratorium)
19-Market Square
20-Ferryman's Tavern
21-Agfa Amphitheatre
22-Victoria Wharf
23-King's Warehouse
24-Red Shed Craft Workshop
25-BMW Pavilion & IMAX Cinema
26-New Somerset Hospital
27-The Portswood Hotel
28-Portswood Square
29-Graduate School of Business
30-Breakwater Lodge
31-Cape Grace Hotel
32-Table Bay Hotel
33-Bascule Bridge
34-Waterfront Visitors Centre

A DIFFICULT CHOICE

The Hildebrand: elegant, cosy dining.
Morton's on the Wharf: Cajun-Creole.
Sports Café: bistro; lots of sports action.
Den Anker: top-class Belgian cuisine.

Arlindo's: delicious seafood or venison.
Greek Fisherman: Mediterranean taverna.
The Musselcracker: traditional seafood.
Aldo's: superb, regional Italian dishes.

Above: *The mood is always festive at the Victoria and Alfred Waterfront which has become one of Cape Town's major drawcards. The universal appeal ensures that its venues bustle with visitors both night and day.*

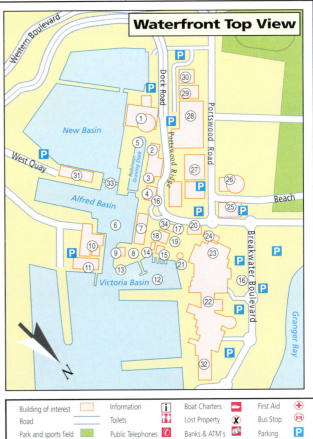

Waterfront Top View

Building of interest		Information		**i** Boat Charters		First Aid
Road		Toilets		Lost Property		Bus Stop
Park and sports field		Public Telephones		Banks & ATM's		Parking

FREE STATE

*T*his semi-arid, mostly flat and treeless central region of South Africa offers the visitor a number of interesting destinations, from game reserves teeming with a variety of wildlife to the ancient, evocative rock paintings along the eastern escarpment. Mine dumps greet your arrival at towns like Welkom, Allanridge and Virginia, all of which sprang up around the latest gold finds, during the years shortly after World War II.

MAIN ATTRACTIONS

Bloemfontein: attractive and vibrant capital of the Free State.
Thaba 'Nchu Sun: lovely hotel and casino complex in the scenic **Maria Moroka National Park** which is a sanctuary for numerous antelope and other wildlife species.
Golden Gate Highlands National Park: scenic wildlife reserve with dramatically sculpted sandstone ridges and cliffs.
The Vaal Dam: 300km² (116-sq-mile) stretch of water, popular with boating enthusiasts and fishermen.
Willem Pretorius Game Reserve: between Winburg and Ventersburg; sustains a variety of wildlife including white rhino, giraffe and buffalo.
Gariep Dam: the country's largest water reservoir; near Bethulie.
Gariep Nature Reserve: located on the vast dam's northern shore; home to a very big population of graceful springbok.

BLOEMFONTEIN	J	F	M	A	M	J	J	A	S	O	N	D
AV. TEMP. °C	23	21	19	15	11	7	7	10	14	17	19	22
AV. TEMP. °F	73	70	66	59	52	45	45	50	57	63	66	72
DAILY SUN hrs	10	9	9	9	9	9	9	9	10	10	10	10
RAINFALL mm	91	99	74	58	21	12	9	14	19	42	59	62
RAINFALL in	4	4	3	2.5	0.8	0.5	0.3	0.6	0.7	2	2.5	2.5

USEFUL CONTACTS

Universitas Hospital,
Bloemfontein, tel: (051) 405-3911.
Bloemfontein Publicity,
tel: (051) 447-1362.
Tourism Northern Cape,
Kimberley, tel: (0531) 3-1434.

DISTANCE IN KM FROM BLOEMFONTEIN	
Aliwal North	207
Bethlehem	239
Cape Town	1004
Kimberley	177
Port Elizabeth	677

ACCOMMODATION

Thaba 'Nchu Sun ★★★★★, tel: (051871) 2161, fax: 2521; hotel and casino complex some 75km (47 miles) east of Bloemfontein.
Welkom Inn ★★★, Welkom, tel: (057) 357-3361, fax: 352-1458.
Gariep Dam Hotel, Gariep Dam, tel: (052172) ask for 60.
Toristo Hotel, Kroonstad, tel: (0562) 2-5111, fax: 3-3298.

TRAVEL TIPS

The Free State's main roads are in good condition, linking this central region with other major South African cities. Please note: distances between towns are vast, so be sure to fill up with petrol regularly.

Below: *This landscape, near Kroonstad, is typical of the Free State. Here, a rain-laden sky dominates the flat terrain punctuated by a solitary windpump.*

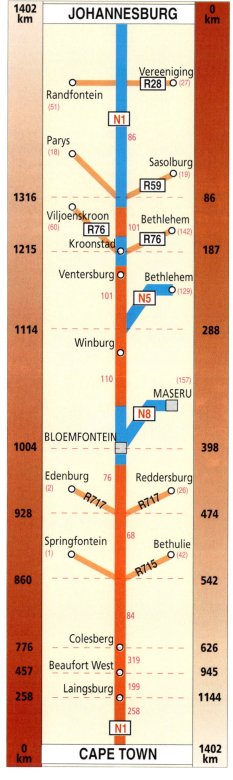

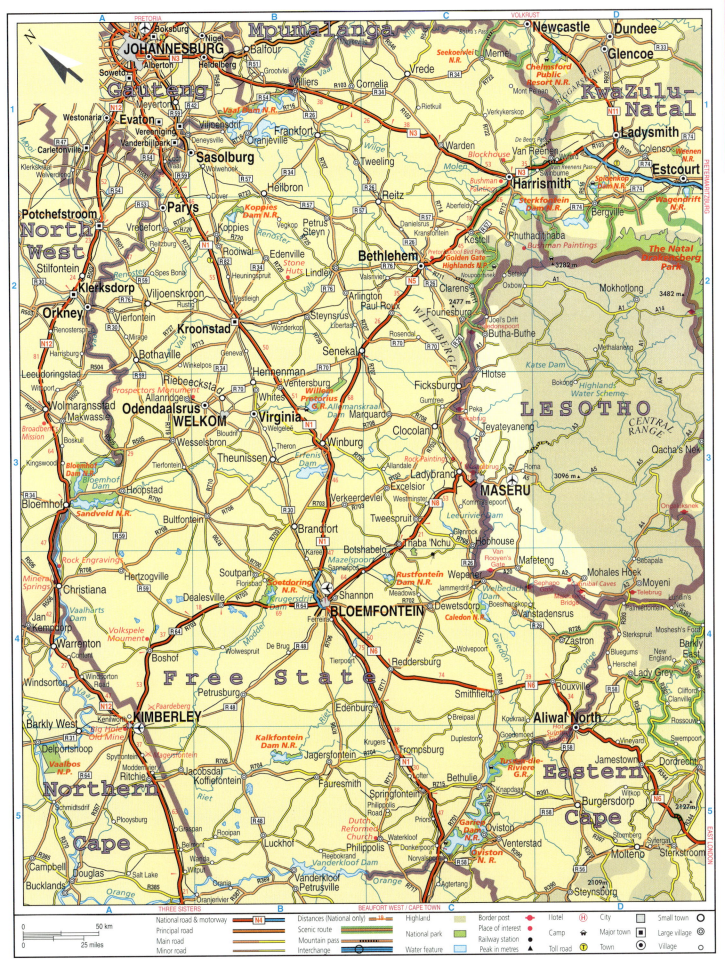

KEY TOURIST AREAS

BLOEMFONTEIN

Bloemfontein is the judicial capital of South Africa and the principal city of the Free State. The most centrally situated of South Africa's major cities, it lies at the heart of an area of fertile farmland 1392m (4567ft) above sea level and owes much of its prosperity to the Free State goldfields located 160km (100 miles) to the northeast. The city is noted for its impressive old buildings, museums, monuments, memorials and public parks and gardens.

MAIN ATTRACTIONS

Franklin Nature Reserve: on Naval Hill; home to a variety of wildlife.
National Botanical Gardens: pleasant floral sanctuary dominated by impressive dolomite outcrops.
Orchid House: pools, waterfalls and over 3000 exquisite orchids at the foot of Naval Hill.
King's Park: visit Loch Logan, the zoo and the beautiful rose garden.
National Women's Memorial: in memory of the more than 27,000 Boer women and children who died in British concentration camps during the Anglo-Boer War.
The Old Raadsaal: the old town hall, housed in a lovely building.
Sand du Plessis Theatre: modern complex; the splendid works of art contribute to the decor.
Soetdoring Nature Reserve: on the R64 to Kimberley; protective habitat for antelope, as well as lion, cheetah and brown hyena.

ACCOMMODATION

Bloemfontein Hotel ★★★★, East Burger Street, tel: (051) 430-1911, fax: 47-7102; in the city centre.
President Hotel ★★★, tel: (051) 430-1111, fax: 430-4141; at the foot of Naval Hill.
Halevy House Hotel ★★, tel: (051) 448-0271, fax: 430-8749; convenient location in the centre of town, close to the museum.

TRAVEL TIPS

Bloemfontein is on the main north–south highway linking Cape Town and Gauteng. Good tarred roads connect the city with all the surrounding major centres, such as Welkom (R700 and R710); Kimberley (R64); Maseru in Lesotho (R64); and East London on the coast (R30).

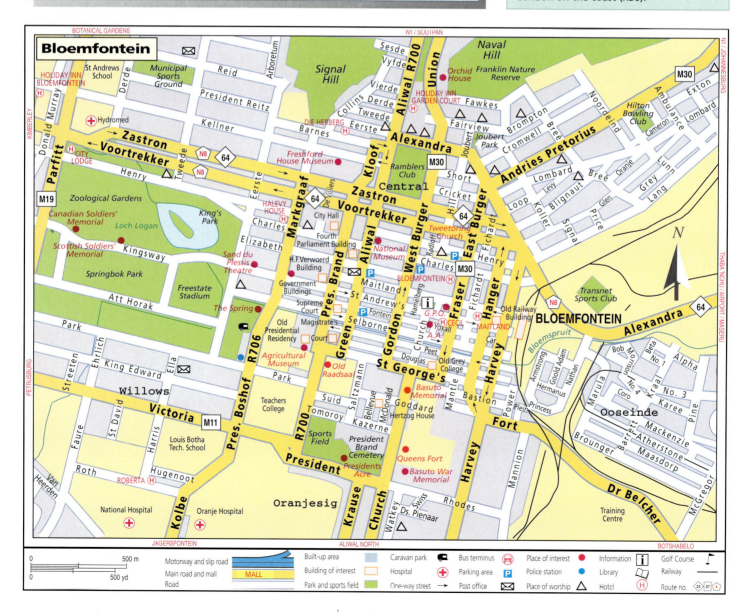

KIMBERLEY

*K*imberley, the diamond town of South Africa and capital of the adjacent Northern Cape province, was born in the 1870s when tens of thousands of prospectors poured into the area to unearth the glittering gems that lay in abundance beneath the dusty ground. Kimberley still retains much of the old-world atmosphere of these heady days, when instant fortunes were made (and lost), and money and champagne flowed like water.

ACCOMMODATION

Holiday Inn Garden Court Kimberley ★★★, tel: (0531) 3-1751, fax: 82-1814; lovely garden setting.
Hotel Kimberlite ★★★, tel: (0531) 81-1966, fax: 81-1967; within easy walking distance of the Big Hole.
Horseshoe Motel, Memorial Road, tel/fax: (0531) 82 5267/8.

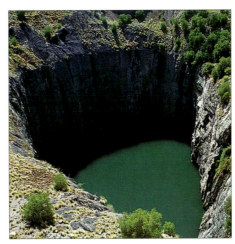

Right: *When diamond fever hit in 1871, no one could have guessed that just 43 years later the dig would have reached a depth of 1097m (3600ft).*

MAIN ATTRACTIONS

The Big Hole: Kimberley's historic hub. By the time it was closed in 1914 it had yielded almost three tons of diamonds.
Kimberley Mine Museum: evocative and comprehensive insight into the town's lively past.
Duggan-Cronin Gallery: an outstanding photographic display of the San-Bushman culture.
William Humphreys Gallery: an excellent collection of South African and European paintings, sculpture and furniture.
The Diggers Fountain: honours the miners who helped to build the Diamond City.
Magersfontein battlefield: call tel: (0531) 3-2645 for directions.

KEY TOURIST AREAS

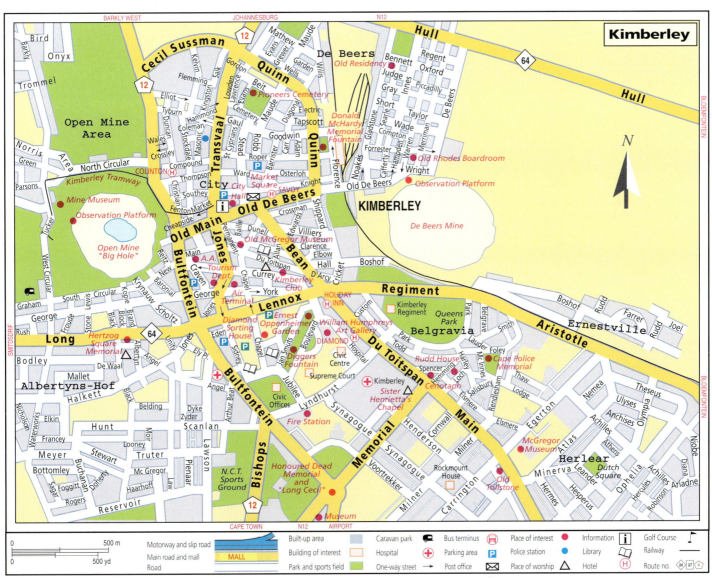

MAIN MAP SECTION KEY AND LEGEND

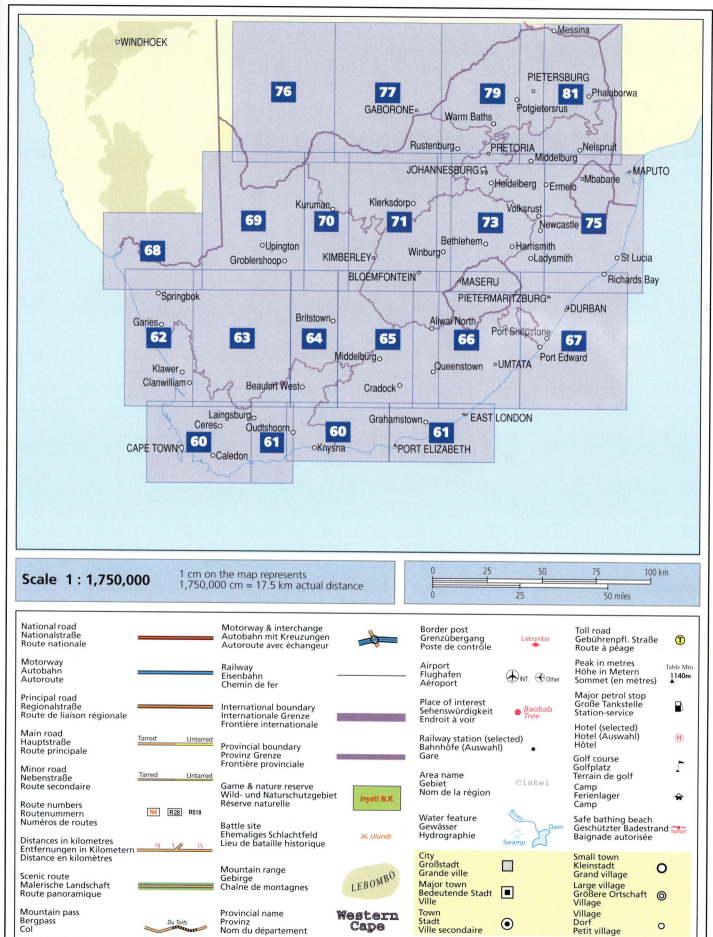

Windhoek

| 76 | 77 | | 79 | 81 |

Messina

PIETERSBURG

Phalaborwa

Potgietersrus

GABORONE

Warm Baths

Rustenburg

PRETORIA

Middelburg · Nelspruit

JOHANNESBURG

Heidelberg · Ermelo · Mbabane · MAPUTO

| 68 | 69 | 70 | 71 | 73 | 75 |

Kuruman · Klerksdorp

Volksrust

Newcastle

Upington

KIMBERLEY

Winburg

Bethlehem

Harrismith

Ladysmith

St Lucia

Groblershoop

BLOEMFONTEIN

MASERU

Richards Bay

PIETERMARITZBURG · DURBAN

Springbok

| 62 | 63 | 64 | 65 | 66 | 67 |

Garies

Britstown

Aliwal North

Port Shepstone

Port Edward

Middelburg

Queenstown · UMTATA

Klawer

Clanwilliam

Beaufort West

Cradock

Laingsburg

Grahamstown · EAST LONDON

Ceres

| 60 | 61 | 60 | 61 |

Oudtshoorn

CAPE TOWN

Caledon

Knysna

PORT ELIZABETH

Scale 1 : 1,750,000

1 cm on the map represents
1,750,000 cm = 17.5 km actual distance

| 0 | 25 | 50 | 75 | 100 km |
| 0 | 25 | | 50 miles | |

National road Nationalstraße Route nationale		Motorway & interchange Autobahn mit Kreuzungen Autoroute avec échangeur		Border post Grenzübergang Poste de contrôle	Lebombo	Toll road Gebührenpfl. Straße Route à péage	T
Motorway Autobahn Autoroute		Railway Eisenbahn Chemin de fer		Airport Flughafen Aéroport	INT. Other	Peak in metres Höhe in Metern Sommet (en mètres)	Table Mtn. ▲ 1140m
Principal road Regionalstraße Route de liaison régionale		International boundary Internationale Grenze Frontière internationale		Place of interest Sehenswürdigkeit Endroit à voir	● Baobab Tree	Major petrol stop Große Tankstelle Station-service	
Main road Hauptstraße Route principale	Tarred Untarred	Provincial boundary Provinz Grenze Frontière provinciale		Railway station (selected) Bahnhöfe (Auswahl) Gare	●	Hotel (selected) Hotel (Auswahl) Hôtel	H
Minor road Nebenstraße Route secondaire	Tarred Untarred	Game & nature reserve Wild- und Naturschutzgebiet Réserve naturelle	Inyati N.R.	Area name Gebiet Nom de la région	Ciskei	Golf course Golfplatz Terrain de golf	
Route numbers Routenummern Numéros de routes	N4 R28 R518	Battle site Ehemaliges Schlachtfeld Lieu de bataille historique	✕ Ulundi	Water feature Gewässer Hydrographie	River Dam Swamp	Camp Ferienlager Camp	
Distances in kilometres Entfernungen in Kilometern Distance en kilomètres	19 15	Mountain range Gebirge Chaîne de montagnes	LEBOMBO			Safe bathing beach Geschützter Badestrand Baignade autorisée	

City
Großstadt
Grande ville · ▢ · Small town
Kleinstadt
Grand village · ○

Major town
Bedeutende Stadt
Ville · ▣ · Large village
Größere Ortschaft
Village · ◎

| Scenic route
Malerische Landschaft
Route panoramique | | Provincial name
Provinz
Nom du département | Western Cape | | | | |
| Mountain pass
Bergpass
Col | Du Toits | | | | | | |

Town
Stadt
Ville secondaire · ◉ · Village
Dorf
Petit village · ○

EASTERN AND WESTERN CAPE

*D*ominated by series after series of soaring mountain ranges, interspersed with rolling wheatfields, orchards and vineyards, the southern part of South Africa is unquestionably one of the country's most beautiful regions. Inland there are forests, deep fertile valleys and spectacular mountain passes to explore, while the rugged, rocky coastline offers the visitor countless venues for safe bathing, surfing, beachcombing and fishing, as well as a number of delightful holiday villages and towns.

MAIN ATTRACTIONS

Wineland towns: wide, tree-lined avenues and beautiful architecture.
Day drives: along the southern coastline; two are particularly recommended: from Cape Town to the little town of Hermanus, haven for southern right whales; and from Cape Town to Lange-baan Lagoon on the West Coast, renowned for its birdlife.
The Garden Route: from Mossel Bay to the Storms River, scenically one of the most splendid parts of the South African coastline; visit Knysna and Plettenberg Bay.
Hex River Valley: dramatic sandstone crags dominate the green, beautiful valley, where excellent grapes are cultivated.
The Little Karoo: a beautiful and rugged region lying between the southern coastal rampart and the Swartberg uplands to the north.

EAST LONDON	J	F	M	A	M	J	J	A	S	O	N	D
AV. TEMP. °C	22	22	21	19	18	16	16	16	17	18	19	21
AV. TEMP. °F	72	72	70	66	64	61	61	61	63	64	66	70
DAILY SUN hrs	7	7	7	7	7	7	8	7	7	7	7	8
RAINFALL mm	74	95	106	80	55	40	51	75	93	95	90	74
RAINFALL in	3	4	4.5	3.5	2.5	2	2.5	3	4	4	4	3.5
SEA TEMP. °C	19	19	19	18	18	17	17	17	17	18	18	18
SEA TEMP. °F	66	66	66	64	64	63	63	63	63	64	64	64

TRAVEL TIPS

The N2 national route leads eastward along the southern coastline from Cape Town to East London, and is the best way to see the beautiful South African countryside. The road is wide and in excellent condition and petrol stations are frequent in the towns it traverses.

LANGEBAAN	J	F	M	A	M	J	J	A	S	O	N	D
AV. TEMP. °C	17	17	17	16	15	14	13	13	14	15	16	17
AV. TEMP. °F	63	63	63	61	59	57	55	55	57	59	61	63
DAILY SUN hrs	7	6	7	7	8	8	7	6	7	7	7	7
RAINFALL mm	3	2	6	15	20	21	22	18	11	8	4	5
RAINFALL in	0.1	0	0.2	0.6	0.8	0.8	0.9	0.7	0.4	0.3	0.1	0.2
SEA TEMP. °C	15	14	13	13	12	12	12	13	13	14	14	14
SEA TEMP. °F	59	57	55	55	54	54	54	55	55	57	57	57

Below: *Countless vineyards were established in the fertile soil of the beautiful Hex River Valley.*

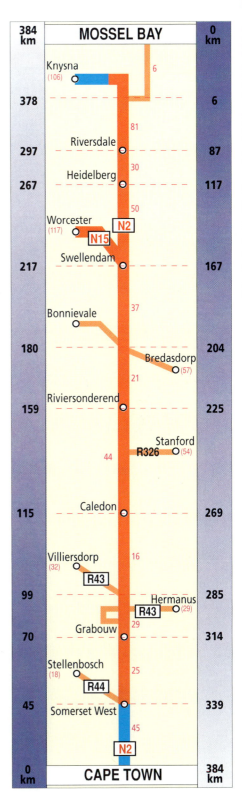

384 km	**MOSSEL BAY**	0 km
	Knysna (106) — 6	
378		6
	81	
297	Riversdale	87
	30	
267	Heidelberg	117
	50	
	Worcester (117) — N2	
	N15	
	Swellendam	167
217		
	37	
	Bonnievale	
180		204
	Bredasdorp (57)	
	21	
	Riviersonderend	225
159		
	Stanford	
	R326 (54)	
	44	
115	Caledon	269
	16	
	Villiersdorp (32)	285
99	R43	
	Hermanus (29)	
	R43	
	Grabouw — 29	314
70		
	Stellenbosch (18)	
	R44 — 25	
45	Somerset West	339
	45	
	N2	
0 km	**CAPE TOWN**	384 km

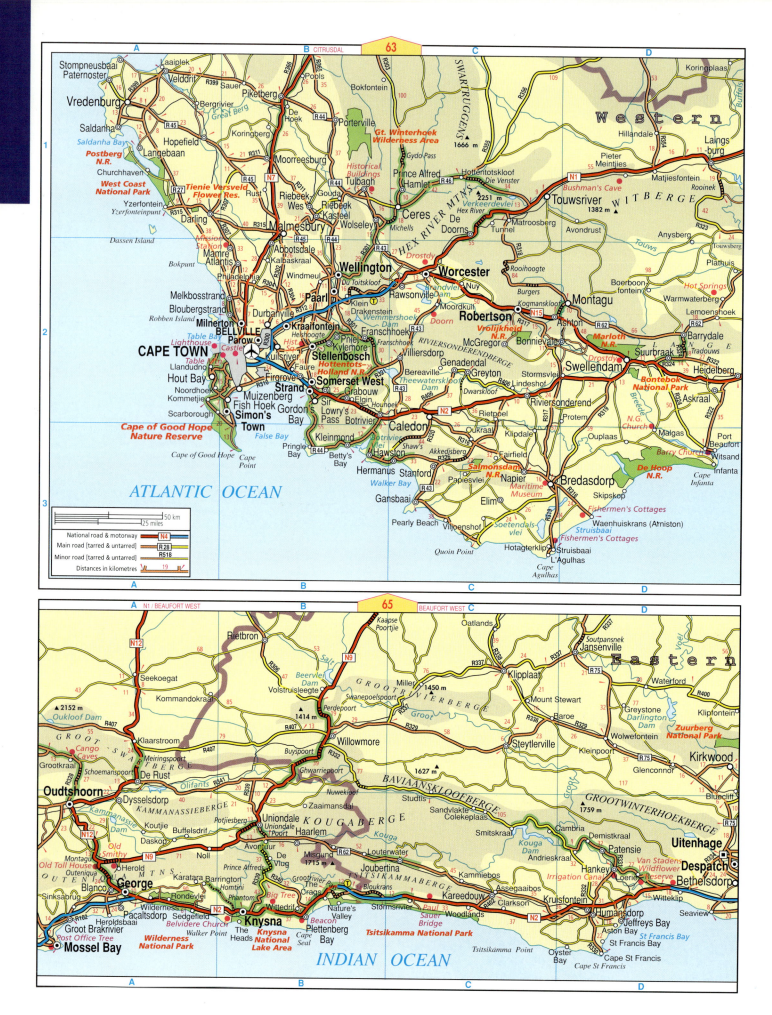

MAIN MAP SECTION

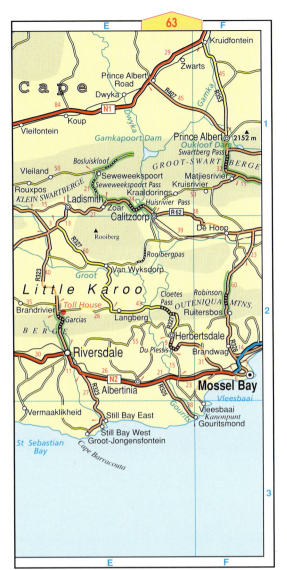

Above: *The scenic splendour of Knysna Lagoon ensured the resort town's popularity and the lagoon is lined with many attractive homes and holiday retreats in garden settings.*

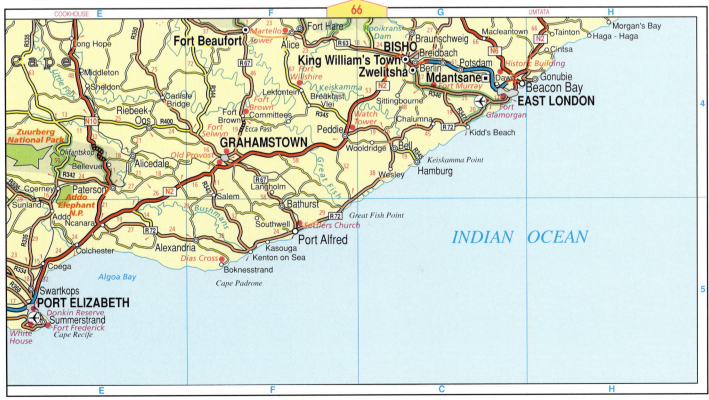

NAMIBIA
BOTSWANA
NORTHERN PROVINCE
Mmabatho · GAUTENG
Pietersburg
Pretoria · · Nelspruit
Johannesburg
NORTH WEST · MPUMALANGA
MOZAMBIQUE
· Upington
FREE STATE · KWAZULU-NATAL
Bloemfontein
NORTHERN CAPE
SOUTH AFRICA
· Durban
EASTERN CAPE
WESTERN CAPE · East London
Cape Town · Port Elizabeth

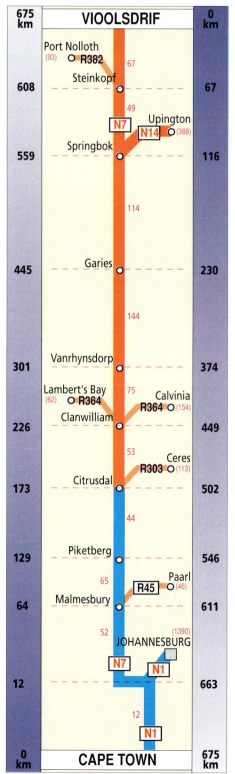

675 km	**VIOOLSDRIF**	0 km
	Port Nolloth (93) ○ R382	
	67	
608	Steinkopf	67
	49	
	N7 Upington	
	N14 ○ (388)	
559	Springbok	116
	114	
445	Garies	230
	144	
301	Vanrhynsdorp	374
	Lambert's Bay (62) ○ R364 Calvinia 75 R364 ○ (154)	
226	Clanwilliam	449
	53 Ceres R303 ○ (113)	
173	Citrusdal	502
	44	
129	Piketberg	546
	65 Paarl R45 ○ (46)	
64	Malmesbury	611
	52 JOHANNESBURG (1390)	
	N7 N1	
12		663
	12 N1	
0 km	**CAPE TOWN**	675 km

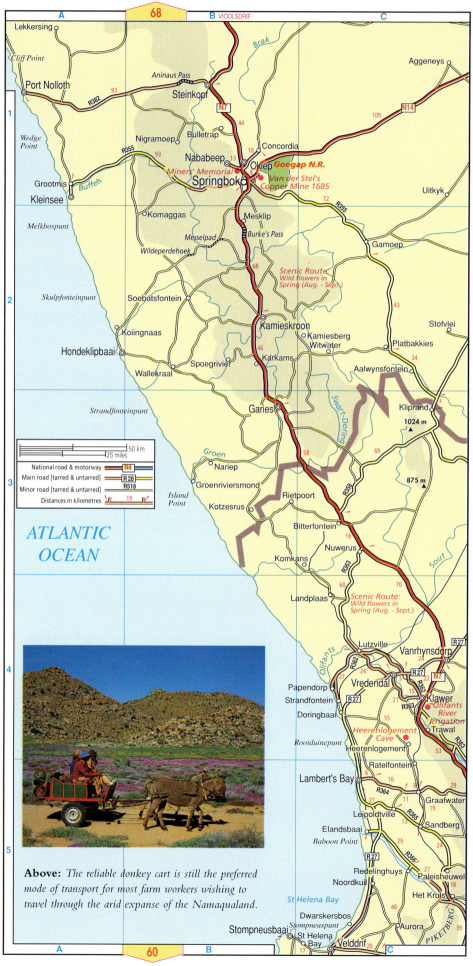

68 VIOOLSDRIF

Lekkersing
Cliff Point
Port Nolloth
R382 · 93
Aninaus Pass
Steinkopf
N7 · 44
Wedge Point
Nigramoep · Bulletrap
Concordia
R355 · 93
Nababeep · 10
13 · Oklep
Miners' Memorial · 8 · Goegap N.R.
Springbok · Van der Stel's Copper Mine 1685
Grootmis
Kleinsee · Buffels
Komaggas · Mesklip
Melkbospunt · Messelpad · Burke's Pass
Wildeperdehoek · 68
Skulpfonteinpunt · Scenic Route: Wild flowers in Spring (Aug. - Sept.)
Soebatsfontein
Koiingnaas · Kamieskroon
Kamiesberg
Witwater
Hondeklipbaai · 46 · Karkams
Spoegrivier
Wallekraal · Karkams
Strandfonteinpunt · Garies
Aggeneys
N14 · 109
Uitkyk
Gamoep
72 · R355
43
Stofvlei
Platbakkies
34
Aalwynsfontein
Kliprand · 3
1024 m
58
875 m
69
R358

ATLANTIC OCEAN

Groen · Nariep
Groenriviersmond
Island Point
Kotzesrus
Rietpoort
Bitterfontein
16
Nuwerus
Komkans
R363 · Sout
Landplaas · 60 · 70
Scenic Route: Wild flowers in Spring (Aug. - Sept.)
Lutzville · Olifants
R362 · Vanrhynsdorp · R27
24 · R27
Papendorp · Vredendal · N7
Strandfontein · R27 · 15
Doringbaai · 21 · Klawer
55 · Olifants River Irrigation
Heerenlogement Cave · Trawal
Rooiduinepunt
Heerenlogement · 53 · R362
Ratelfontein
Lambert's Bay · 16
R364 · 11 · Graafwater
Leipoldtville · 19
13 · Sandberg
Elandsbaai · 29
Baboon Point · R27
Redelinghuys · 27
Noordkuil · R366 · 24
St Helena Bay · Paleisheuwel
Het Kruis · 18
Dwarskersbos · 48
Stompneuspunt
Stompneusbaai · St Helena Bay
Aurora · 39
60 · Velddrif · 20
17

	National road & motorway	N4
	Main road [tarred & untarred]	R 28
	Minor road [tarred & untarred]	R518
	Distances in kilometres	19

50 km / 25 miles

Above: The reliable donkey cart is still the preferred mode of transport for most farm workers wishing to travel through the arid expanse of the Namaqualand.

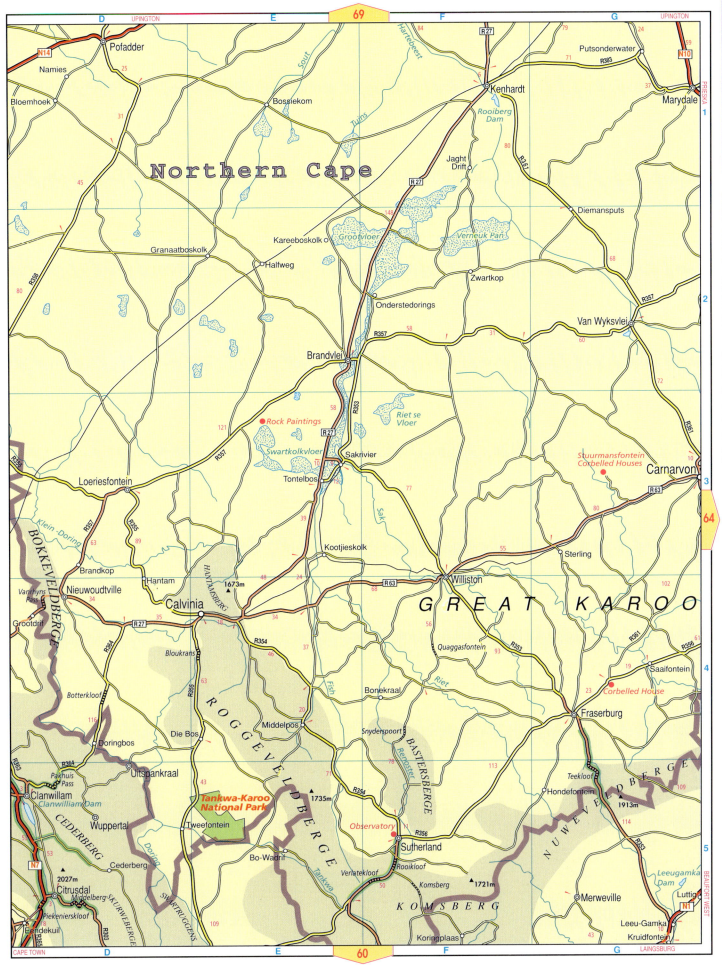

GREAT KAROO

*T*his hauntingly beautiful, semi-arid region of bone-dry air, minimal rainfall and intense sunshine dominates the Cape interior. The landscape consists of largely featureless countryside stretching endlessly to the distant horizons, lonely windmills, a few isolated farmsteads, and flocks of sheep sustained by underground water.

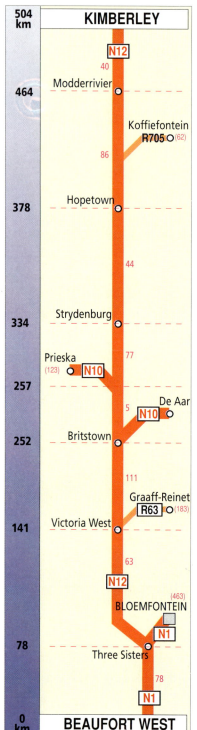

MAIN ATTRACTIONS

Beaufort West: birthplace of the famed heart surgeon Chris Barnard, this little town is also noted for its lovely, pear-tree-lined streets.

Karoo National Park: north of Beaufort West; wildlife includes Cape mountain zebra, shy leopard and a variety of antelope.

Graaff-Reinet: third-oldest town in the Cape, with some fine old architecture.

Valley of Desolation: near Graaff-Reinet; a fantasia of wind-eroded, strangely shaped dolerite peaks, pillars and balancing rocks.

Nieu-Bethesda: tiny hamlet, 50km (31 miles) north of Graaff-Reinet; home to the Owl House museum's bizarre sculptures, many of which are decorated with ground glass.

Cradock: in the vicinity are the Mountain Zebra National Park and well-known author Olive Schreiner's grave.

Aliwal North: this pleasant town to the far east of the Great Karoo has hot sulphur springs and an excellent spa.

TRAVEL TIPS

The main highways that traverse the vast Karoo region, and those servicing the northern and north-western Cape are generally in good condition. Note: be sure to stop for petrol and refreshments in good time, as the towns (and the service stations) tend to lie rather far apart in this area.

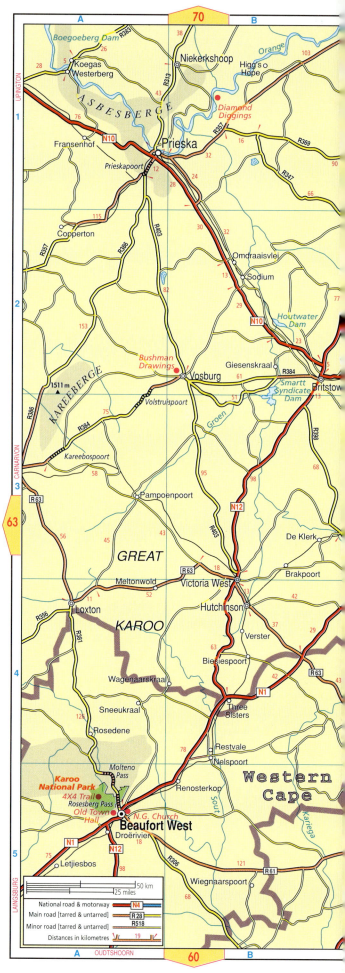

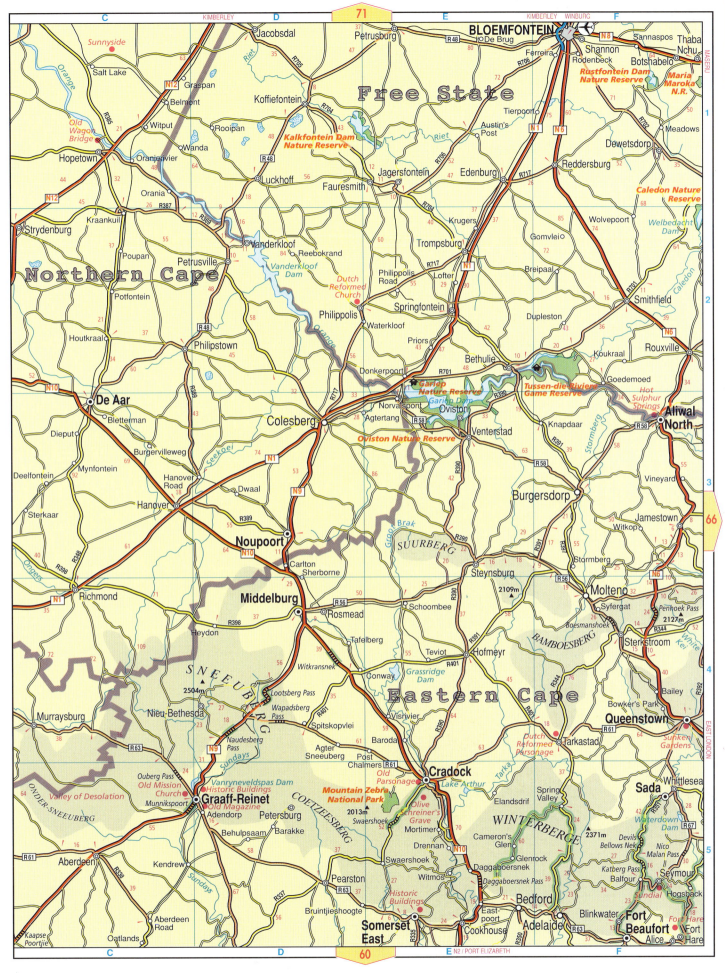

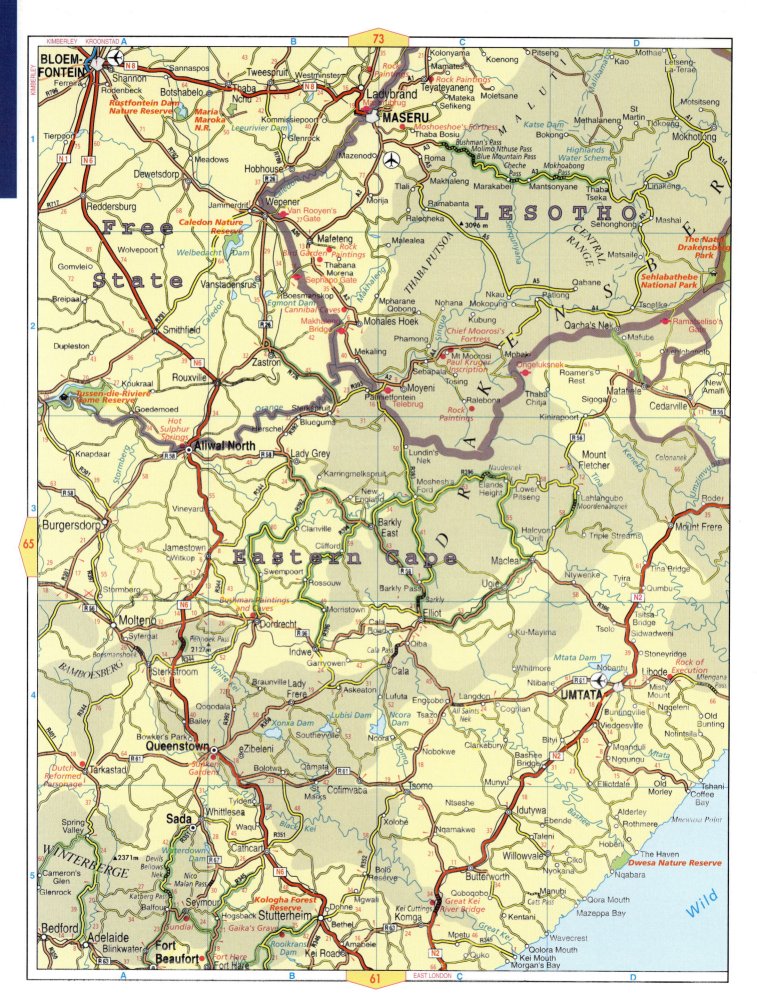

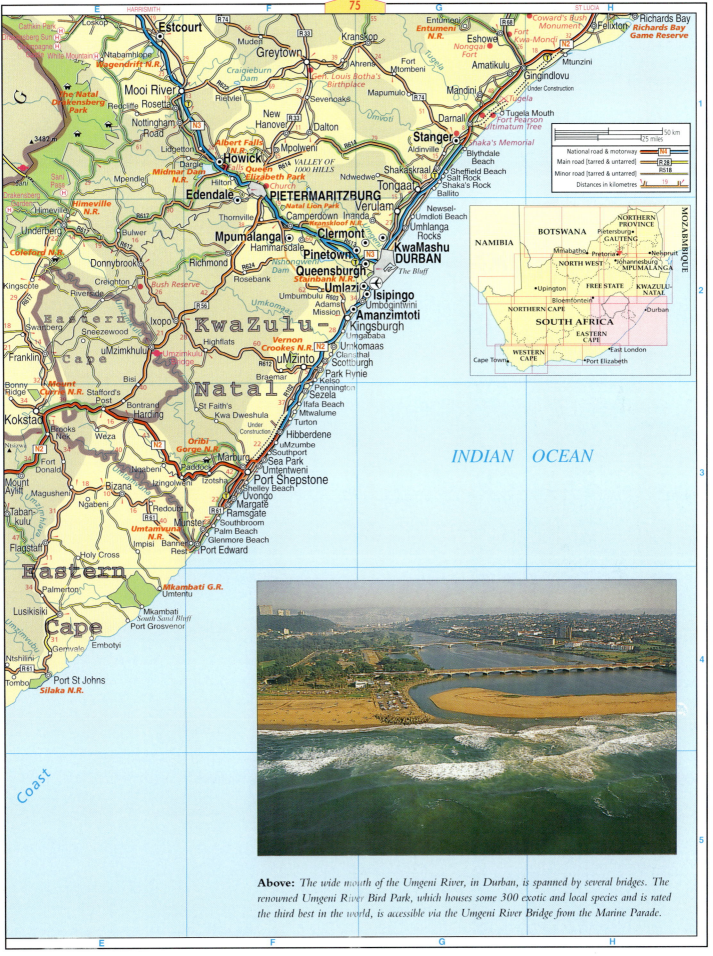

75

MAIN MAP SECTION

Above: *The wide mouth of the Umgeni River, in Durban, is spanned by several bridges. The renowned Umgeni River Bird Park, which houses some 300 exotic and local species and is rated the third best in the world, is accessible via the Umgeni River Bridge from the Marine Parade.*

NORTHERN CAPE

This is a dry, rather forbidding moonscape of low mountains and strange plants like the kokerboom. After the rainy season, however, the arid veld is transformed into a riot of colour as wildflowers bloom in abundance. Towns are few and small, with the exception of Upington, which is beautifully situated along the banks of the Orange River.

DISTANCE IN KM FROM UPINGTON	
Bloemfontein	588
Cape Town	894
Kimberley	411
Windhoek (Namibia)	1005

TRAVEL TIPS

Remember: towns (and service stations) are set rather far apart. Beware of wild animals crossing the road, especially at dawn, dusk and through the night.

MAIN ATTRACTIONS

Upington: visit one of the dried fruit co-ops around the town.
Augrabies Falls National Park: marvel at the lovely waterfall (one of the five biggest in the world) in this otherwise harsh area, and take a drive through the reserve to spot the bird- and wildlife.
Kalahari Gemsbok National Park: located on the Botswana border, 280km (108 miles) north of Upington. Red sand dunes, oryx (gemsbok), shy Kalahari lion, an abundance of raptor species, and magnificent sunsets attract nature lovers to this unique desert park.
Goegap Nature Reserve: east of Springbok; spot eland, springbok and mountain zebra along hiking trails and game drives.
Richtersveld National Park: in the far northwestern corner of the province; excellent game-viewing.
Vioolsdrif/Noordoewer: South Africa/Namibia border post, for travellers heading to Namibia.

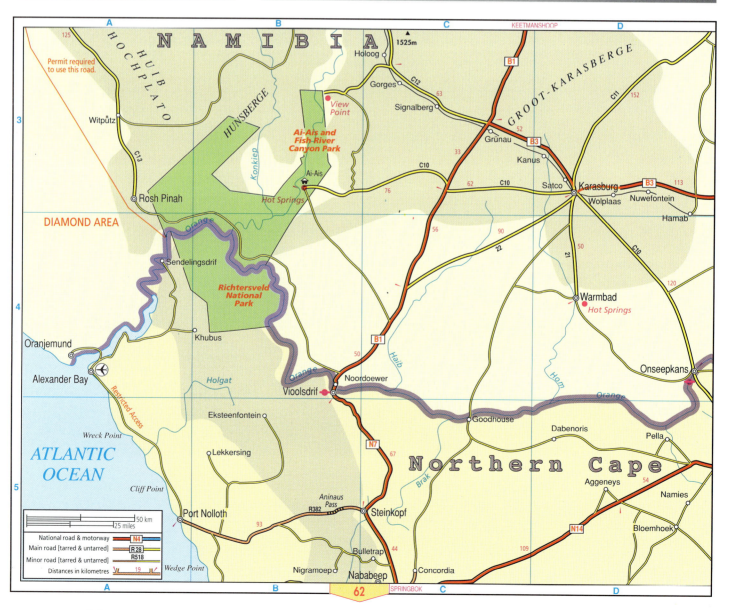

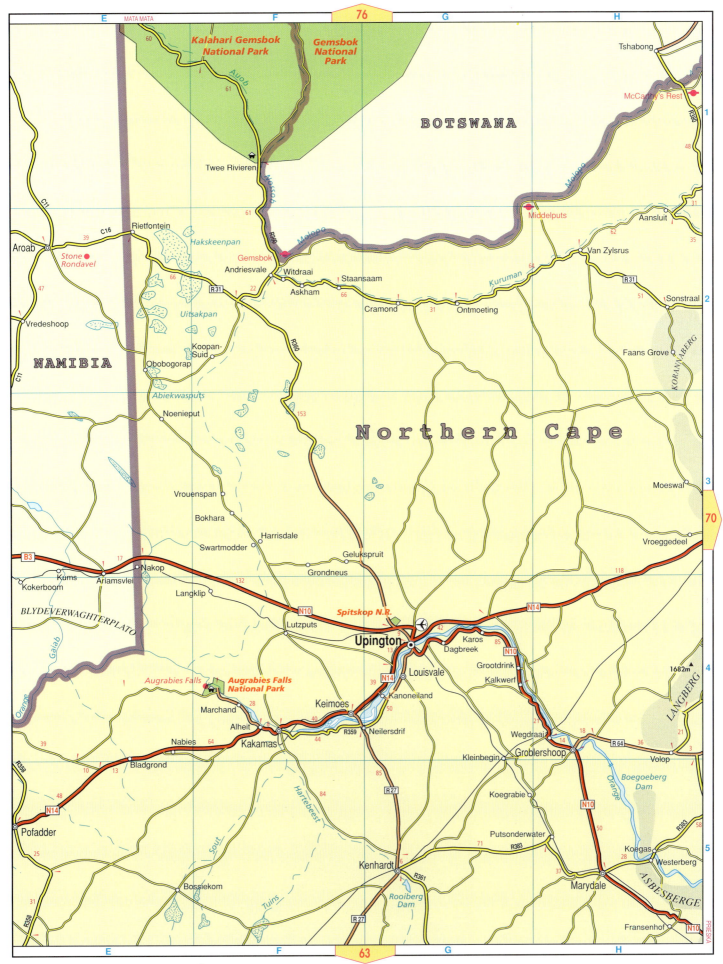

MAIN MAP SECTION

KIMBERLEY AND BLOEMFONTEIN

*T*hese neighbouring towns, the capitals of the Northern Cape and Free State provinces respectively, are situated on the high interior plateau. Both towns offer many interesting museums and lovely sandstone buildings of historical interest and are surrounded by nature reserves and dams.

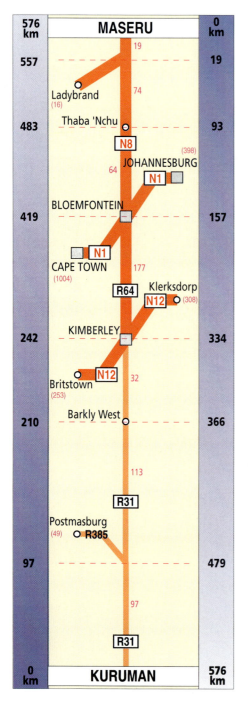

Above: The statue of Christiaan Rudolph De Wet stands in front of the classic sandstone structure of the Fourth Raadsaal, the last government seat of the old Republic.
Below: The Kimberley Diamond Mine Museum portrays life on the diamond fields 100 years ago.

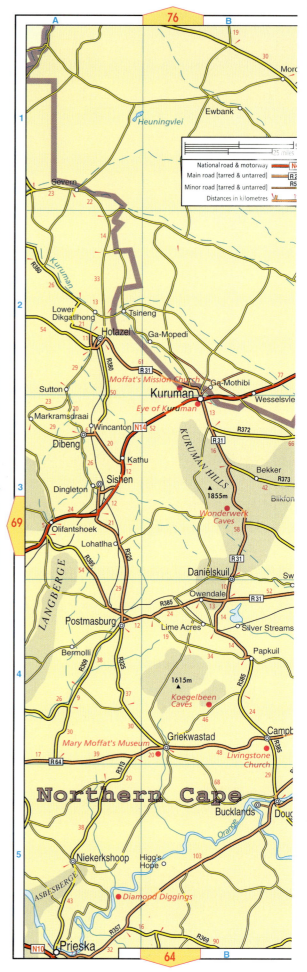

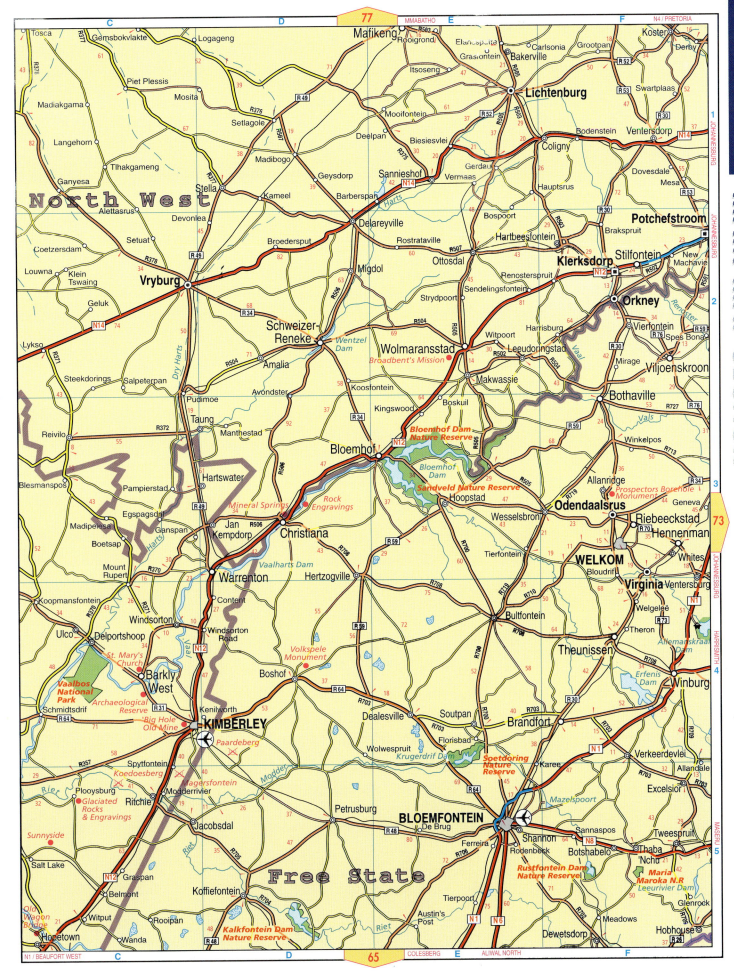

NORTHEASTERN FREE STATE

*T*hough much of the Free State consists of flat, treeless grassland plain, the eastern and southern parts are scenically very appealing, rising in a series of picturesquely weathered sandstone hills, and culminating in the Maluti Mountains in the southeastern corner. The northeastern part of the province is blessed with rich farmland, making the Free State one of the most important agricultural areas of the country. The province is also rich in deposits of gold ore estimated to be worth in the region of 8,5 billion rand.

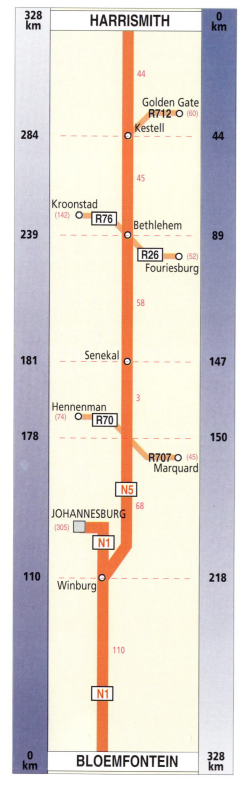

MAIN ATTRACTIONS

Golden Gate Highlands National Park: south of Bethlehem; sandstone ridges sculpted by the elements; see antelope and over 160 bird species.
Vaal River: border between Free State and Gauteng; good boating and fishing, especially on the dam.

Willem Pretorius Game Reserve: good game-viewing, including white rhino and buffalo, near Ventersburg.
Pretoriuskloof Bird Park: located near the little town of Bethlehem.
Bushman paintings: in the Phuthaditjhaba area, close to Lesotho.

BETHLEHEM	J	F	M	A	M	J	J	A	S	O	N	D
AV. TEMP. °C	19	19	18	14	10	6	7	9	13	16	18	19
AV. TEMP. °F	66	66	64	57	50	43	45	48	55	61	64	66
DAILY SUN hrs	9	8	8	8	9	8	9	9	9	8	9	9
RAINFALL mm	120	89	71	50	28	10	11	14	33	67	85	97
RAINFALL In	5	4	3	2	1	0.4	0.4	0.6	1	3	3.5	4

Below: *Along the Free State roads, travellers are often greeted by large fields of glorious golden-yellow sunflowers. These constitute a major crop in the region which has rich soil, despite relatively poor rainfall and very little surface water.*

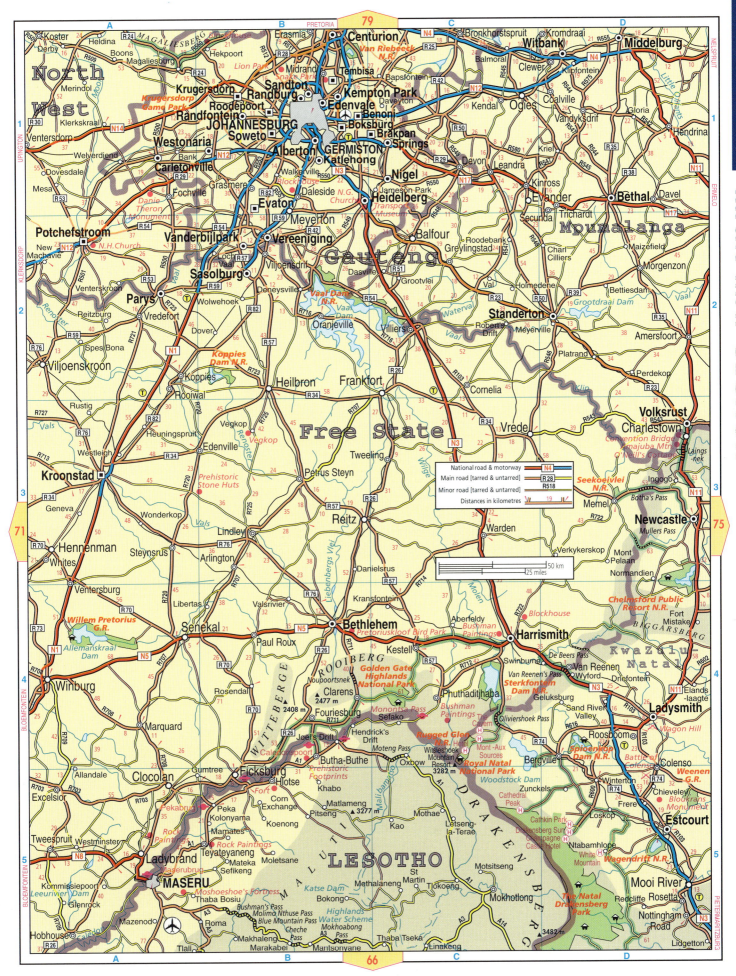

National road & motorway	N4
Main road [tarred & untarred]	R28
Minor road [tarred & untarred]	R518
Distances in kilometres	19

50 km
25 miles

NORTHERN KWAZULU-NATAL

The midlands and northern parts of KwaZulu-Natal, overlooked by the Drakensberg massif to the west, are noted for their rolling green hills, rich farmlands, charming country towns – and for their place in the military annals. For much of the 1800s this region served as an immense battleground as three nations fought bitterly for mastery of the land. Closer to the coast lie the splendours of the Greater St Lucia Wetland Park and some of Africa's very finest wildlife reserves. The seaboard offers superb angling and boating, while offshore the world's southernmost coral reefs are guaranteed to delight scuba divers.

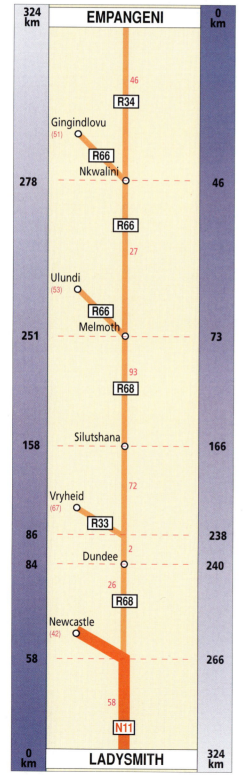

324 km	EMPANGENI	0 km
	46	
	R34	
	Gingindlovu (51)	
	R66	
278	Nkwalini	46
	R66	
	27	
	Ulundi (53)	
	R66	
251	Melmoth	73
	93	
	R68	
158	Silutshana	166
	72	
	Vryheid (67)	
	R33	
86		238
	2	
84	Dundee	240
	26	
	R68	
	Newcastle (42)	
58		266
	58	
	N11	
0 km	LADYSMITH	324 km

Above: *The Itala Game Reserve, a 30,000ha (74,000-acre) wildlife sanctuary located along the lush banks of the Pongola River, is a haven for the white, or square-lipped, rhino, a highly endangered species. The term 'white' derives from the Afrikaans word 'wyd' (wide) describing the broad, squarish mouth of this mammal.*

RICHARDS BAY	J	F	M	A	M	J	J	A	S	O	N	D
AV. TEMP. °C	25	25	25	23	20	18	17	19	20	21	23	25
AV. TEMP. °F	77	77	77	73	68	64	63	66	68	70	73	77
DAILY SUN hrs	7	7	7	8	8	7	8	8	7	6	7	7
RAINFALL mm	144	138	110	111	126	31	47	59	84	97	97	83
RAINFALL in	6	5.5	4.5	4.5	5	1	2	2.5	3.5	4	4	3.5
SEA TEMP. °C	24	24	24	23	22	21	20	20	20	21	21	23
SEA TEMP. °F	75	75	75	73	72	70	68	68	68	70	70	73

MAIN ATTRACTIONS

Howick Falls: outside of Howick, the Umgeni River plunges some 100m (328ft) into a rock pool.
Hluhluwe/Umfolozi Park: the oldest of South Africa's wildlife sanctuaries, this park sustains a great number of animals and some 400 species of bird.
Itala Game Reserve: home to some 70 species of mammal, among them both white and black rhino, zebra, giraffe, elephant, brown hyena, cheetah and various antelope. Beautiful Ntshondwe rest camp is just one accommodation alternative that is available here.
Phinda Resource Reserve: an upmarket ecotourist venture that shares its resources with the local communities, while providing the visitor with an exhilarating wilderness experience.

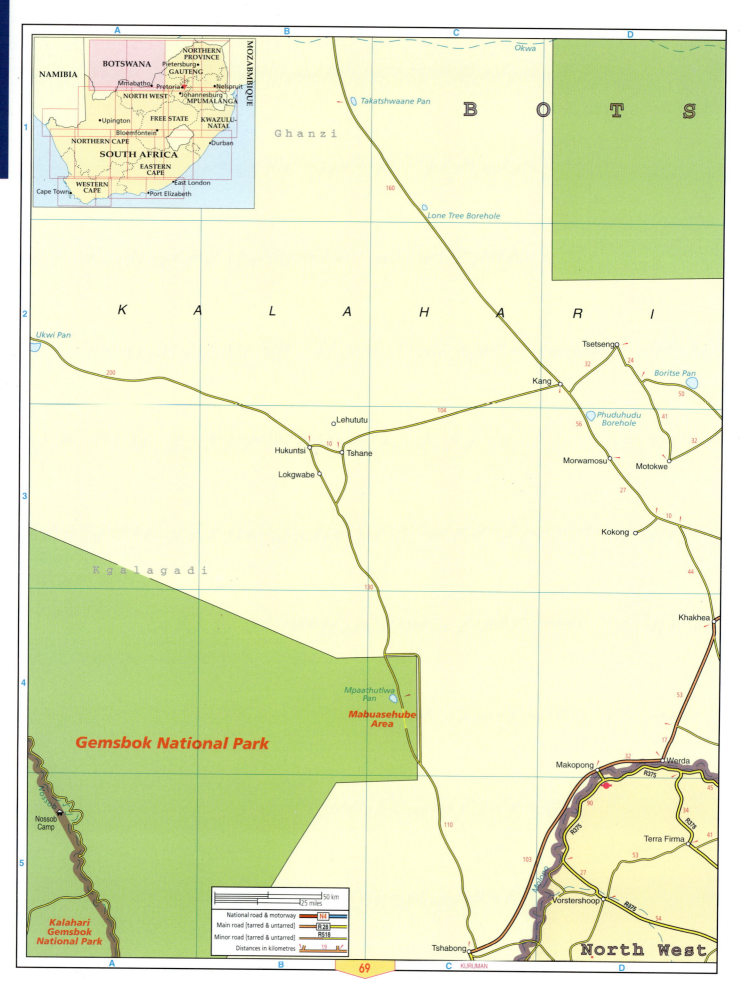

NAMIBIA

BOTSWANA

NORTHERN PROVINCE

Pietersburg

GAUTENG

Mmabatho Pretoria Nelspruit

Johannesburg MPUMALANGA

NORTH WEST

MOZAMBIQUE

Upington FREE STATE KWAZULU-NATAL

Bloemfontein Durban

NORTHERN CAPE

SOUTH AFRICA

EASTERN CAPE

WESTERN CAPE East London

Cape Town Port Elizabeth

Okwa

B O T S

Takatshwaane Pan

Ghanzi

160

Lone Tree Borehole

K A L A H A R I

Ukwi Pan

200

Tsetsengo

32 24

Boritse Pan

Kang

104

50

Phuduhudu Borehole

56 41

Lehututu

32

Hukuntsi 10 Tshane

Morwamosu Motokwe

Lokgwabe

27

Kgalagadi

Kokong 10

44

130

Khakhea

53

Mpaathutlwa Pan

17

Mabuasehube Area

Gemsbok National Park

32 Werda

Makopong R375

Nossob

45

90

R375 34 R378

Nossob Camp

Terra Firma 41

110

103 53

27

Kalahari Gemsbok National Park

Molopo

Vorstershoop R375

54

50 km

25 miles

National road & motorway N4

Main road [tarred & untarred] R28

Minor road [tarred & untarred] R518

Distances in kilometres 19

Tshabong **North West**

A B **69** C KURUMAN D

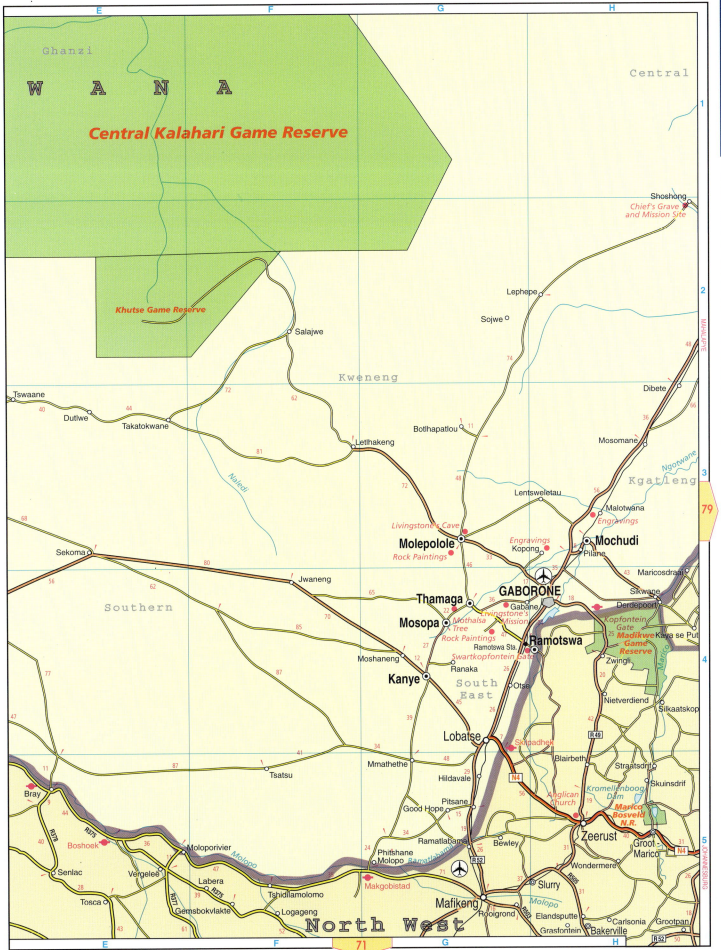

Central

Ghanzi

W A N A

Central Kalahari Game Reserve

Khutse Game Reserve

Shoshong
*Chief's Grave
and Mission Site*

Lephepe

Sojwe

Salajwe

Kweneng

Dibete

Tswaane

40

Dutlwe

44

Takatokwane

72

62

Botlhapatlou

11

Mosomane

Ngotwane

Kgatleng

Letlhakeng

72

Naledi

81

48

Lentsweletau

56

Malotwana
Engravings

Sekoma

68

80

Livingstone's Cave

Molepolole
Rock Paintings

46

33

Engravings
Kopong

Pilane

Mochudi

35

Maricosdraai

Sikwane

Derdepoort

Jwaneng

65

Thamaga

36

Gabane

GABORONE

17

18

43

*Kopfontein
Gate*

*Madikwe
Game
Reserve*

Kaya se Put

56

62

70

22

Mosopa
*Mothalsa
Tree
Rock Paintings*

*Livingstone's
Mission*

47

25

Southern

85

27

Ramotswa

Ramotswa Sta.
Swartkopfontein Gate

Zwingli

Moshaneng

12

Ranaka

26

20

77

87

Kanye

45

South
East

Otse

Nietverdiend

Silkaatskop

39

26

R 49

42

Lobatse

7

Skipadhek

Blairbeth

Straatsdrif

Skuinsdrif

47

34

48

Mmathethe

29

N4

11

87

Tsatsu

Hildavale

*Kromellenboog
Dam*

Bray

9

44

Pitsane

56

*Anglican
Church*

19

**Marico
Bosveld
N.R.**

Good Hope

Ramatlabama

Bewley

Zeerust

**Groot
Marico**

N4

R375

R378

Boshoek

36

Moloporivier

Molopo

Phitshane
Molopo

Ramatlabama

71

R 52

31

Wondermere

R506

26

Senlac

Vergelee

Labera

R375

Makgobistad

Slurry

31

Tosca

Gemsbokvlakte

Tshidilamolomo

Mafikeng

Rooigrond

R506

Elandsputte

Carlsonia

Grootpan

Logageng

52

North West

Grasfontein

Bakerville

R 52

50

NORTH WEST AND NORTHERN PROVINCE

*T*he *North West is a vast, hot, flattish country of bushveld and thorn, of lonely farmsteads, of fields of sunflowers, groundnuts, tobacco, and citrus, and of villages that sleep soundly in the sun. This is one of the great granaries of southern Africa, with endless fields of maize stretching out to the far horizon. Scattered over this region and across the more densely populated Northern Province to the northeast is an impressive number of natural and man-made attractions well worth travelling to from the main centres of Pretoria and Johannesburg.*

TRAVEL TIPS

All national roads in this area are tarred and generally in excellent condition; most of the secondary roads are gravelled and reasonably well maintained.

Please note: The stretch of road between Warm Baths and Pietersburg can get very busy over the Easter weekend. Holiday-makers travelling to the towns and game reserves of the Lowveld join a cavalcade of minibus taxis and public buses ferrying worshippers of the ZCC (Zionist Christian Church) to their destination on the outskirts of Pietersburg. Traffic is congested and extreme caution is advised.

DISTANCE IN KM FROM PRETORIA	
Klerksdorp	164
Messina	530
Pietersburg	319
Rustenburg	125
Witbank	92

MAIN ATTRACTIONS

Sun City and Palace of the Lost City: luxury hotel-casino complex of pure innovation and fantasy.
Pilanesberg National Park: great expanse of wildlife-rich habitat.
Warm Baths: renowned for its curative springs; the Hydro Spa is of world standard.
Pietersburg: principal town of the Northern Province; nearby are the **Percy Fyfe Nature Reserve**, where several antelope species may be seen, and the interesting **Bakone Malapa Open-air Museum**, with traditional *kraal* and handicrafts.

Below: *The natural springs at Warm Baths are not the only attraction at this world-class spa resort.*

Route strip map

492 km	BEIT BRIDGE	0 km
476	Messina — 16	16
	92	
384	Louis Trichardt — N1	108
	117	
	Tzaneen (95) — R71	
267	Pietersburg	225
	57	
	Zebediela R518 (42)	
210	Potgietersrus	282
	51	
	Roedtan N11 (39)	
159	Naboomspruit	333
	58	
	Warm Baths (3) R516	
101		391
	101	
0 km	PRETORIA	492 km

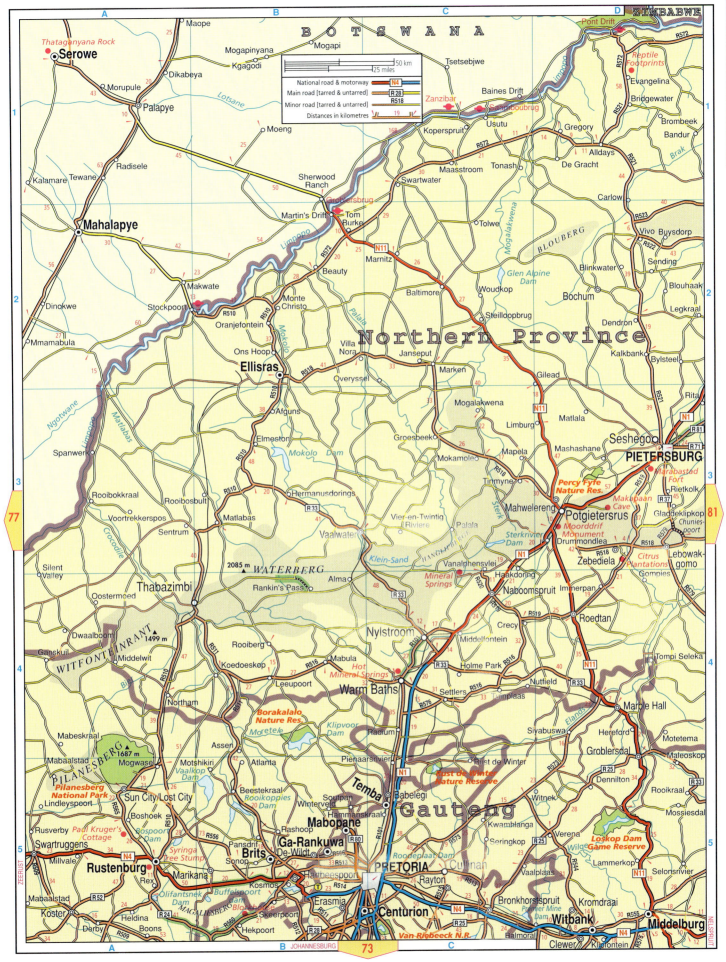

NORTHERN PROVINCE AND MPUMALANGA

*M*uch of this region is dominated by the Great Escarpment, a spectacular compound of forest-mantled mountains, deep ravines, crystal-clear streams and delicate waterfalls. For sheer scenic beauty, few other parts of the country can compare with this imposing range, which rises near Nelspruit and runs to the northeast for some 300km (186 miles). To the east of the escarpment lies the wildlife-rich Lowveld, where the vast Kruger National Park and a host of beautiful private reserves are situated.

436 km	PIETERSBURG	0 km
	N1	
	57	
Tom Burke (178)	N11	
	Potgietersrus	
379		57
PRETORIA (216)	N1	
	74	
	N11	
305		131
	16	
289	Marble Hall	147
	21	
268	Groblersdal	168
	78	
190	Middelburg	246
	5	
	N11	
PRETORIA (140)	N4	
185		251
	N12	
JOHANNESBURG (170)		
	55	
	Belfast (2)	
	R33	
130		306
	37	
93	Waterval-Boven	343
	93	
	N4	
0 km	NELSPRUIT	436 km

MAIN ATTRACTIONS

Pilgrim's Rest: a living showcase of the early gold-mining days.
Zebediela: South Africa's largest citrus estates are located here.
Pietersburg: this is the principle town of the Northern Province.
Tzaneen: little town surrounded by lovely waterfalls and forests. Visit nearby **Duiwelskloof** and **Magoebaskloof** and see the realm of the mysterious **Modjadji Rain Queen** (the source for Sir Rider Haggard's classic novel *She*) and the impressive cycad forest.
Loskop Dam Game Reserve: a wildlife sanctuary around a large dam; accommodation is offered in several air-conditioned chalets.

Below: *The Blyde River winds its way through the magnificent canyon of the same name.*

PIETERSBURG	J	F	M	A	M	J	J	A	S	O	N	D
AV. TEMP. °C	22	22	20	18	15	12	12	14	17	20	21	22
AV. TEMP. °F	72	72	68	64	59	54	54	57	63	68	70	72
DAILY SUN hrs	8	8	8	8	9	9	9	9	9	9	8	8
RAINFALL mm	91	72	61	31	11	4	5	4	14	41	80	91
RAINFALL in	4	3	2.5	1	0.4	0.1	0.2	0.1	0.6	2	3.5	4

TRAVEL TIPS

Most of the roads are tarred and generally in excellent condition and well signposted. The climate is equable, though rainfall during the summer months, from November to February, often occurs in the form of sudden torrential downpours which are accompanied by thunder and lightning. The storms tend to be brief, however, and there are very few days without long hours of sunshine.
A common feature of the escarpment is the occurrence of dense fog patches, and caution is therefore advised.
During the previous century, malaria claimed the lives of many pioneers in this area. While the disease is under control today thanks to insecticides, it is essential to take precautionary measures before travelling into the region.

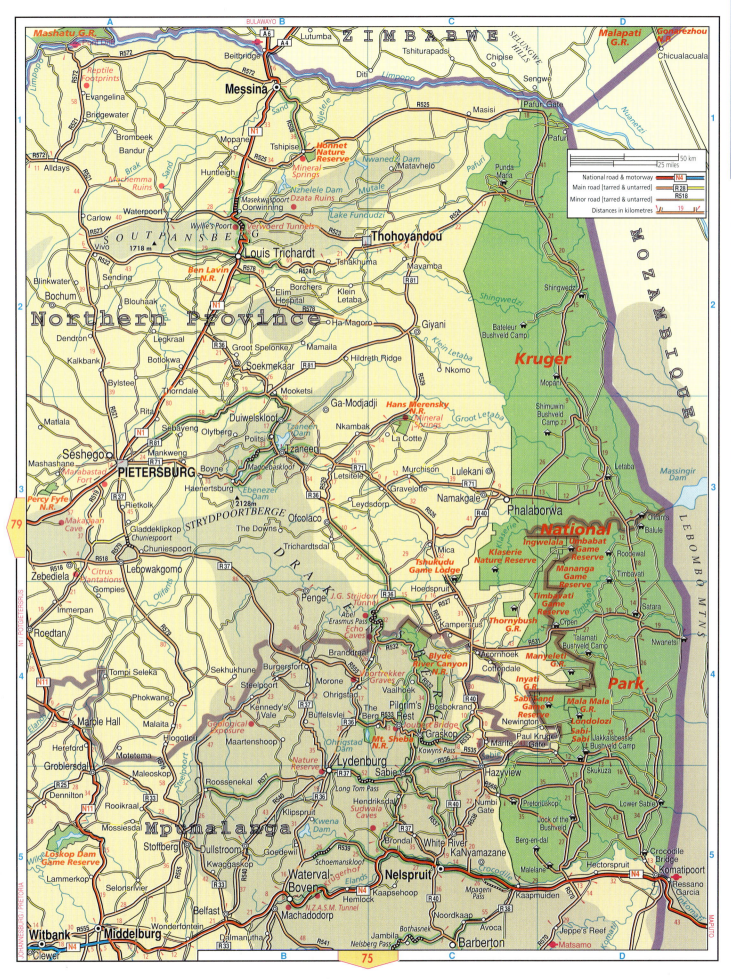

MAIN MAP SECTION

KEY TOURIST AREA AND TEXT INDEX

Note: Numbers in **bold** denote photographs

Place	Ref	Page
Colchester	C3	34
Coldstream	G2	39
Colenso	C2	31
	A3	32
Colenso	D1	55
Committees	E2	35
Commondale	C1	32
Constantia		46
Content	A4	55
Cookhouse	C1	34
Coombs	E2	35
Cornelia	B1	55
Cottondale	C4	21
	D1	22
Cradock		64
Craigsforth	D1	31
Crossroads	F2	35
Curry's Post	D4	31
Dalmanutha	B2	22
Dalton	B3	32
Damwal	A2	22
Danielsrus	C2	55
Dannhauser	A2	32
Dargle	C5	31
Darling	B5	45
Darnall	A5	25
	C3	32
Daskop	C1	38
De Brug	B4	55
De Hoek	B4	45
De Vlug	E2	39
Dealesville	B4	55
Deepdale	C5	31
Delportshoop	A5	55
Demistkraal	A3	34
Deneysville	A1	55
Dennitlon	A2	22
Despatch	B4	34
Dewetsdorp	C4	55
Die Hoek	D2	39
Dimbaza	F1	35
Diphuti	B3	21
Dlolwana	B3	32
Dlomodlomo	A1	25
Donkerpoort	C5	55
Dordrecht	D5	55
Doringbaai	B3	45
Doringbos	C3	45
Douglas	A5	55
Dover	B1	55
Drakensberg		**30**
Driefontein	A2	32
Dublin	B3	21
Dududu	B3	27
Dullstroom	B2	22
Dundee	B2	32
	D1	55
Dupelston	C5	55
Durban		**67**
Golden Mile		**28**
Dwarskersbos	B4	45
Dwarsrand	A1	25
Dysselsdorp	B1	38
East London	G2	35
East Poort	C1	34
Edenburg	C4	55
Edendale	A1	27
Edendale	D5	31
Edenville	B2	55
Edinglassie	B1	27
Eendekuil	C4	45
Ekuseni	C1	25
Ekutuleni	A4	25
Elandsbaai		45
	B3	45
Elandshoek	B5	21
Elandskraal	B2	32
Elandslaagte	A2	32
elephant		**20**
Elliot	B1	33
Elliotdale	B2	33
embassies (international)		16
Embotyi	C2	33
Empangeni	B4	25
	D3	32
Enon	B3	34
Entumeni	A4	25
	C3	32
eNyamazaneni	D2	22
Escombe	C1	27
Eshowe	A4	25
	C3	32
Esikhawini	B4	25
Esperanza	B3	27
Estcourt	C3	31
	A3	32
	D1	55
Eston	B1	27
Evaton	A1	55
Excelsior	C3	55
Fallodon	F3	35
Fauresmith	B5	55
Felixton	B4	25
	D3	32
Ferreira	B4	55
Ficksburg	C3	55
Fitzsimon's Snake Park		28
Flagstaff	C2	33
Florisbad	B4	55
Forestry Station	B3	34
Fort Beaufort	E1	35
Fort Brown	E2	35
Fort Donald	D1	33
Fort Frederick		36
Fort Hare	E1	35
Fort Mtombeni	C3	32
Fouriesburg	C2	55
Frankfort	F1	35
	B1	55
Franklin	D1	33
Frasers Camp	E2	35
FREE STATE		**54**, **72**
Frere	A3	32
Garies	A1	45
Garryowen	A1	33
Geluksburg	B1	31
Gemvale	C2	33
Geneva	B2	55
George	B2	38
		40
Gingindlovu	A5	25
	C3	32
Gladstone	F1	35
Glen Beulah	A3	27
Glen Echo	B3	27
Glenashley	D1	27
Glencoe	A2	32
	D1	55
Glenconnor	B3	34
Glenmore Beach	A5	27
	D2	33
Glenrock	C3	55
Glentana	B3	38
Gluckstadt	C2	32
God's Window		22
Goedemoed	C5	55
Goedewil	B2	22
Gold Reef City		12
Golden Valley	C1	34
Gompies	A1	22
Gonubie	G2	35
Gonzana	E1	35
Gqweta	B4	21
Graaff-Reinet		64
Graafwater	B3	45
Grahamstown		**35**
	D2	35
Graskop	B4	21
	C1	22
Graspan	A5	55
Greystone	A2	34
Greytown	B3	32
Groblersdal	A1	22
Groenriviersmond	A1	45
Groenvlei	B1	32
Groot-Brakrivier	A3	38
Grootdrif	C2	45
Grootspruit	B1	32
Grootvlei	B1	55
Gumtree	C3	55
Haarlem	E1	39
Haga-Haga	A2	33
Halcyon Drift	C1	33
Hamburg	F2	35
Hankey	A4	34
Hantam	C2	45
Harding	D1	33
Harper	E2	35
Harrisburg	A2	55
Harrismith	B1	31
	C1	55
Hartebeespoort Dam		10
Hartenbos	A3	38
Hattingspruit	A2	32
Hazyview	C4	21
	D1	22
Hectorspruit	D5	21
	D2	22
Heerenlogement	B3	45
Heidelberg	B1	55
Heilbron	B1	55
Helpmekaar	B2	32
Hemlock	C2	22
Hendriksdal	B5	21
	C2	22
Hennenman	B3	55
Hereford	A1	22
Hermanus		59
Herold	B2	38
Heroldsbaai	B3	38
Herschel	D4	55
Hertzogville	A4	55
Het Kruis	B4	45
Heuningspruit	B2	55
Hex River Valley		**42**
Hibberdene	B4	27
Hibberds	B4	25
high commissions (international)		16
Highflats	A3	27
Highveld		10
Hillcrest	C1	27
Himeville	B5	31
Hlabisa	B2	25
	D2	32
Hlobane	C1	32
Hlogotlou	B1	·22
Hlomela	B1	21
Hlotse	C2	55
Hluhluwe	C2	25
	D2	32
Hlutankungu	A3	27
Hobeni	B2	33
Hobhouse	C3	55
Hoedspruit	B3	21
Hoekwil	C2	38
Hogsback		35
	E1	35
Hole-in-the-Wall		33
Holy Cross	C2	33
Hoopstad	A3	55
Hopefield	B4	45
Hopewell	B2	34
Hornlee	D3	39
hospitals		
Bloemfontein		54
Cape Town		49
Durban		28
Johannesburg		10
Knysna		41
Nelspruit		23

MAIN MAP INDEX

Name	Grid	Page	Name	Grid	Page	Name	Grid	Page	Name	Grid	Page
Cala	C4	66	Colesberg	D3	65	Dibete	H3	77	Erasmia	B1	73
Cala Road	C4	66	Coligny	F1	71	Die Bos	E4	63	Ermelo	A2	75
Caledon	C2	60	Committees	F4	61	Diemansputs	G2	63	Escourt	E1	67
Calitzdorp	E2	61	Commondale	B3	75	Dieput	C3	65	Eshowe	G1	67
Calvert	B4	75	Concordia	B1	62	Dikabeya	A1	79	Evander	C1	73
Calvinia	E4	63	Content	D4	71	Dingleton	A3	70	Evangelina	D1	79
Cambria	C5	60	Conway	D4	65	Dinokwe	A2	79	Evaton	B1	73
Cameron's Glen	E5	65	Cookhouse	E5	65	Dirkiesdorp	A2	75	Ewbank	B1	70
Campbell	B4	70	Copperton	A2	64	Diti	C1	81	Excelsior	F5	71
Camperdown	F2	67	Corn Exchange	B5	73	Dohne	B5	66	eZibeleni	B4	66
Candover	C3	75	Cornelia	C2	73	Donkerpoort	E2	65	Faans Grove	H2	69
Cape St Francis	D5	60	Cottondale	C4	81	Donnybrook	E2	67	Fairfield	C3	60
Cape Town	A2	60	Cradock	E5	65	Dordrecht	B4	66	Faure	B2	60
Carletonville	A1	73	Cramond	G2	69	Doringbaai	C4	62	Fauresmith	E1	65
Carlisle Bridge	E4	61	Crecy	C4	79	Doringbos	D4	63	Felixton	H1	67
Carlow	D1	79	Creighton	E2	67	Douglas	B5	70	Ferreira	F1	65
Carlton	D3	65	Crocodile Bridge	D5	81	Dover	B2	73	Ficksburg	B5	73
Carnarvon	G3	63	Croydon	C1	75	Dovesdale	F1	71	Firgrove	B2	60
Carolina	A1	75	Cullinan	C5	79	Drennan	E5	65	Fish Hoek	B2	60
Carsonia	E1	71	Dabenoris	D5	68	Driefontein	D4	73	Flagstaff	E3	67
Catembe	D1	75	Dagbreek	G4	69	Droërivier	A5	64	Florisbad	E4	71
Cathcart	B5	66	Daggaboersnek	E5	65	Drummondlea	D3	79	Fochville	A1	73
Catuane	D2	75	Daleside	B1	73	Duiwelskloof	B3	81	Forbes Reef	B1	75
Cedarville	D2	66	Dalmanutha	A1	75	Dullstroom	B5	81	Fort Beaufort	F4	61
Cederberg	D5	63	Dalton	F1	67	Dundee	A4	75	Fort Brown	F4	61
Centurion	B1	73	Daniëlskuil	B3	70	Dupleston	F2	65	Fort Donald	E3	67
Ceres	C1	60	Danielsrus	B3	73	Durban	G2	67	Fort Hare	F4	61
Chalumna	G4	61	Dannhauser	A4	75	Durbanville	B2	60	Fort Mistake	D4	73
Changalane	C1	75	Dargle	F1	67	Dutlwe	E3	77	Fort Mtombeni	G1	67
Charl Cilliers	D2	73	Darling	A1	60	Dwaal	D3	65	Fouriesburg	B4	73
Charlestown	D3	73	Darnall	G1	67	Dwaalboom	A4	79	Frankfort	C2	73
Chicabela	D1	75	Daskop	A5	60	Dwarskersbos	C5	62	Franklin	E2	67
Chicualacuala	D1	81	Dasville	C2	73	Dwyka	E1	61	Franschhoek	B2	60
Chieveley	D5	73	Davel	D1	73	Dysselsdorp	A5	60	Fransenhof	A1	64
Chipise	C1	81	Daveyton	C1	73	East London	G4	61	Fraserburg	G4	63
Chrissiesmeer	A1	75	Dawn	G4	61	Eastpoort	E5	65	Frere	D5	73
Christiana	D3	71	De Aar	C3	65	Ebende	C5	66	Ga-Modjadji	B3	81
Chuniespoort	A3	81	De Brug	E1	65	Edenburg	E1	65	Ga-Mopedi	B2	70
Churchhaven	A1	60	De Doorns	C1	60	Edendale	F1	67	Ga-Mothibi	B2	70
Ciko	D5	66	De Gracht	D1	79	Edenvale	B1	73	Ga-Rankuwa	B5	79
Cintsa	H4	61	De Hoek	B1	60	Edenville	B3	73	Gabane	G4	77
Citrusdal	D5	63	De Hoop	F2	61	Eendekuil	D5	63	Gaborone	H4	77
Clansthal	F2	67	De Klerk	B3	64	Egspagsdrif	C3	71	Gamoep	C2	62
Clanville	B3	66	De Rust	A4	60	Eksteenfontein	B5	68	Gansbaai	C3	60
Clanwilliam	D5	63	De Vlug	B5	60	Elands Height	C3	66	Ganskuil	A4	79
Clarens	C4	73	De Wildt	B5	79	Elandsbaai	C5	62	Ganspan	C3	71
Clarkebury	C4	66	Dealesville	E4	71	Elandsdrif	E5	65	Ganyesa	C1	71
Clarkson	C5	60	Deelfontein	C3	65	Elandskraal	A4	75	Garies	B3	62
Clermont	G2	67	Deelpan	E1	71	Elandslaagte	D4	73	Garryowen	B4	66
Clewer	D1	73	Delareyville	D2	71	Elandsputte	E1	71	Gege	B2	75
Clifford	B3	66	Delportshoop	C4	71	Elgin	B2	60	Geluk	C2	71
Clocolan	A5	73	Demistkraal	D5	60	Elim	C3	60	Geluksburg	D4	73
Coalville	D1	73	Dendron	D2	79	Elim Hospital	B2	81	Gelukspruit	F3	69
Coega	E5	61	Deneysville	B2	73	Elliot	C4	66	Gemsbokvlakte	C1	71
Coerney	E4	61	Dennilton	D5	79	Elliotdale	D4	66	Gemvale	E4	67
Coetzersdam	C2	71	Derby	F1	71	Ellisras	B2	79	Genadendal	C2	60
Coffee Bay	D5	66	Derdepoort	H4	77	Elmeston	B3	79	Geneva	F3	71
Cofimvaba	B4	66	Despatch	D5	60	Emangusi	D2	75	George	A5	60
Coghlan	C4	66	Devon	C1	73	Embotyi	E4	67	Gerdau	E1	71
Colchester	E5	61	Devonlea	D2	71	Empangeni	C5	75	Germiston	B1	73
Colekeplaas	C5	60	Dewetsdorp	F1	65	Engcobo	C4	66	Geysdorp	D1	71
Colenso	D5	73	Dibeng	A3	70	Entumeni	G1	67	Giesenskraal	B2	64

Gilead	D2	79	Haenertsburg	B3	81	Hluthi	C3	75	Kalamare	A1	79
Gingindlovu	G1	67	Haga-Haga	H4	61	Hobeni	D5	66	Kalbaskraal	B2	60
Giyani	C2	81	Halfweg	E2	63	Hobhouse	B1	66	Kalkbank	D2	79
Gladdeklipkop	D3	79	Halycon Drift	D3	66	Hoedspruit	C4	81	Kalkwerf	G4	69
Glencoe	A4	75	Hamab	D3	68	Hofmeyr	E4	65	Kameel	D1	71
Glenconnor	D4	60	Hamburg	G4	61	Hogsback	F5	65	Kamiesberg	C2	62
Glenmore Beach	F3	67	Hammarsdale	F2	67	Holbank	A2	75	Kamieskroon	B2	62
Glenrock	B1	66	Hankey	D5	60	Holme Park	C4	79	Kampersrus	C4	81
Glenrock	E5	65	Hanover	C3	65	Holmedene	C2	73	Kang	D2	76
Gloria	D1	73	Hanover Road	D3	65	Holoog	C3	68	Kanoneiland	G4	69
Gluckstadt	B4	75	Hantam	D4	63	Holy Cross	E3	67	Kanus	D3	68
Goba	C1	75	Harding	E3	67	Hondefontein	G5	63	Kanye	G4	77
Goedemoed	F2	65	Harrisburg	F2	71	Hondeklipbaai	A2	62	Kao	D1	66
Goedewil	B5	81	Harrisdale	F3	69	Hoopstad	E3	71	Karasburg	D3	68
Golela	C3	75	Harrismith	C4	73	Hopefield	A1	60	Karatara	A5	60
Gompies	D4	79	Hartbeesfontein	F2	71	Hopetown	C1	65	Karee	E5	71
Gomvlei	F2	65	Hartbeeskop	B1	75	Hotagterklip	C3	60	Kareeboskolk	E2	63
Gonubie	H4	61	Hartbeespoort	B5	79	Hotazel	A2	70	Kareedouw	C5	60
Good Hope	G5	77	Hartswater	D3	71	Hottentotskloof	C1	60	Karkams	B2	62
Goodhouse	C5	68	Hattingspruit	A4	75	Hout Bay	A2	60	Karos	G4	69
Gordon's Bay	B2	60	Hauptrus	E1	71	Houtkraal	C2	65	Karringmelkspruit	B3	66
Gorges	C3	68	Hawston	B3	60	Howick	F1	67	Kasouga	F5	61
Gouda	B1	60	Hazyview	C5	81	Hukuntsi	B3	76	Kathu	A3	70
Gouritsmond	F3	61	Hectorspruit	D5	81	Humansdorp	D5	60	Katlehong	B1	73
Graaff-Reinet	D5	65	Heerenlogement	C4	62	Huntleigh	B1	81	Kaya se Put	H4	77
Graafwater	C5	62	Heidelberg	B1	73	Hutchinson	B4	64	Keate's Drift	A5	75
Grabouw	B2	60	Heidelberg	D2	60	Idutywa	C5	66	Kei Mouth	C5	66
Grahamstown	F4	61	Heilbron	B2	73	Ifafa Beach	F3	67	Kei Road	B5	66
Granaatboskolk	E2	63	Hekpoort	B1	73	Immerpan	D4	79	Keimoes	F4	69
Grasfontein	E1	71	Heldina	A1	73	Impisi	E3	67	Kelso	F2	67
Graskop	C4	81	Helpmekaar	A4	75	Inanda	G2	67	Kempton Park	B1	73
Grasmere	B1	73	Hemlock	B5	81	Indwe	B4	66	Kendal	C1	73
Graspan	C1	65	Hendrick's Drift	B4	73	Infanta	D3	60	Kendrew	C5	65
Gravelotte	C3	81	Hendriksdal	C5	81	Ingogo	D3	73	Kenhardt	F1	63
Gregory	D1	79	Hendrina	D1	73	Ingwavumba	C3	75	Kenilworth	D4	71
Greylingstad	C2	73	Hennenman	F3	71	Inhaca	D1	75	Kennedy's Vale	B4	81
Greystone	D4	60	Herbertsdale	E2	61	Isipingo	G2	67	Kentani	C5	66
Greyton	C2	60	Hereford	D4	79	Iswepe	A2	75	Kenton on Sea	F5	61
Greytown	F1	67	Herefords	C1	75	Itsoseng	E1	71	Kestell	C4	73
Griekwastad	B4	70	Hermanus	C3	60	Ixopo	E2	67	Kgagodi	B1	79
Groblersdal	D5	79	Hermanusdorings	B3	79	Izingolweni	E3	67	Khabo	B5	73
Groblershoop	H4	69	Herold	A5	60	Izotsha	F3	67	Khakhea	D4	76
Groenriviersmond	B3	62	Heroldsbaai	A5	60	Jacobsdal	C5	71	Khubus	B4	68
Groenvlei	A3	75	Herschel	B3	66	Jagersfontein	E1	65	Kidds Beach	G4	61
Groesbeek	C3	79	Hertzogville	D3	71	Jaght Drift	F1	63	Kimberley	C4	71
Grondneus	F3	69	Het Kruis	C5	62	Jambila	B1	75	King William's Town	G4	61
Groot Brakrivier	A5	60	Heuningspruit	A3	73	Jameson Park	C1	73	Kingsburgh	F2	67
Groot Spelonke	B2	81	Heydon	D4	65	Jamestown	F3	65	Kingscote	E2	67
Groot-Marico	H5	77	Hibberdene	F3	67	Jammerdrif	B1	66	Kingsley	A3	75
Grootdrif	D4	63	Higg's Hope	B1	64	Jan Kempdorp	D3	71	Kingswood	E3	71
Grootdrink	G4	69	Highflats	F2	67	Jansenville	D4	60	Kinirapoort	D2	66
Grootkraal	A4	60	Hildavale	G5	77	Janseput	C2	79	Kinross	C1	73
Grootmis	A1	62	Hildreth Ridge	B2	81	Jeffreys Bay	D5	60	Kirkwood	D4	60
Grootpan	F1	71	Hillandale	D1	60	Jeppe's Reef	C1	75	Klaarstroom	A4	60
Grootspruit	A3	75	Hilton	F1	67	Joel's Drift	B4	73	Klawer	C4	62
Grootvlei	C2	73	Himeville	E2	67	Johannesburg	B1	73	Klein Drakenstein	B2	60
Grünau	C3	68	Hlabisa	C4	75	Joubertina	C5	60	Klein Letaba	B2	81
Gt-Jongensfontein	E3	61	Hlathikhulu	B2	75	Jozini	C3	75	Klein Tswaing	C2	71
Gumtree	A5	73	Hlobane	B3	75	Jwaneng	F4	77	Kleinbegin	G4	69
Ha-Magoro	B2	81	Hlogotlou	A4	81	Kaapmuiden	C5	81	Kleinmond	B3	60
Haakdoring	C3	79	Hlotse	B5	73	Kaapsehoop	C5	81	Kleinpoort	D4	60
Haarlem	B5	60	Hluhluwe	C4	75	Kakamas	F4	69	Kleinsee	A1	62

Name	Grid	Page	Name	Grid	Page	Name	Grid	Page	Name	Grid	Page
Klerksdorp	F2	71	Kwaggaskop	B5	81	Lofter	E2	65	Maloma	C2	75
Klerkskraal	A1	73	KwaMashu	G2	67	Logageng	C1	71	Malotwana	H3	77
Klipdale	C3	60	KwaMbonambi	C4	75	Lohatlha	A3	70	Mamaila	B2	81
Klipfontein	D1	73	Kwamhlanga	C5	79	Lokgwabe	B3	76	Mamates	C1	66
Klipfontein	D4	60	Kylemore	B2	60	Long Hope	E4	61	Mamre	B2	60
Klipplaat	C4	60	L'Agulhas	C3	60	Loskop	E1	67	Mandini	G1	67
Kliprand	C3	62	La Cotte	C3	81	Lothair	A1	75	Mangeni	A4	75
Klipspruit	B5	81	Laaiplek	A1	60	Louis Trichardt	B2	81	Manhoca	D2	75
Knapdaar	F3	65	Labera	F5	77	Louisvale	G4	69	Mankayane	B2	75
Knysna	B5	60	Ladismith	E1	61	Louterwater	B5	60	Mankweng	A3	81
Koedoeskop	B4	79	Lady Frere	B4	66	Louwna	C2	71	Manthestad	D3	71
Koegas	A1	64	Lady Grey	B3	66	Louwsburg	B3	75	Mantsonyane	C1	66
Koegrabie	G5	69	Ladybrand	B1	66	Lower Dikgatlhong	A2	70	Manubi	D5	66
Koenong	C1	66	Ladysmith	D4	73	Lower Pitseng	C3	66	Manzini	B2	75
Koffiefontein	D1	65	Lahlangubo	D3	66	Loxton	A4	64	Maope	A1	79
Koiingnaas	A2	62	Laingsburg	D1	60	Loyengo	B2	75	Mapela	C3	79
Kokerboom	E4	69	Lambert's Bay	C5	62	Luckhoff	D1	65	Mapumulo	G1	67
Kokong	D3	76	Lammerkop	D5	79	Lufuta	C4	66	Maputo	D1	75
Kokstad	E3	67	Landplaas	C4	62	Lulekani	C3	81	Marakabei	C1	66
Kolonyama	C1	66	Langberg	E2	61	Lundin's Nek	C3	66	Marble Hall	D4	79
Komaggas	B2	62	Langdon	C4	66	Luneberg	A3	75	Marburg	F3	67
Komatipoort	D5	81	Langebaan	A1	60	Lusikisiki	E4	67	Marchand	F4	69
Komga	C5	66	Langehorn	C1	71	Luttig	G5	63	Margate	F3	67
Komkans	C3	62	Langholm	F4	61	Lutumba	B1	81	Maricosdraai	H4	77
Kommandokraal	A4	60	Langklip	F4	69	Lutzputs	F4	69	Marikana	B5	79
Kommetjie	A2	60	Lavumisa	C3	75	Lutzville	C4	62	Marite	C4	81
Kommissiepoort	B1	66	Leandra	C1	73	Lydenburg	B5	81	Marken	C2	79
Koopan-Suid	F2	69	Lebowakgomo	D3	79	Lykso	C2	71	Markramsdraai	A3	70
Koopmansfontein	C4	71	Leeu-Gamka	G5	63	Maartenshoop	B4	81	Marnitz	C2	79
Koosfontein	D2	71	Leeudoringstad	E2	71	Maasstroom	C1	79	Marquard	A4	73
Kootjieskolk	E3	63	Leeupoort	B4	79	Mabaalstad	A5	79	Marracuene	D1	75
Koperspruit	C1	79	Legkraal	A2	81	Mabeskraal	A4	79	Martin's Drift	B2	79
Kopong	H3	77	Lehlohonolo	D2	66	Mabopane	B5	79	Marydale	G1	63
Koppies	A2	73	Lehututu	B3	76	Mabula	B4	79	Maseru	B1	66
Koringberg	B1	60	Leipoldtville	C5	62	Machadodorp	B5	81	Mashai	D1	66
Koringplaas	F5	63	Lekfontein	F4	61	Machava	D1	75	Mashashane	D3	79
Kosmos	B5	79	Lekkersing	A1	62	Macleantown	G4	61	Masisi	C1	81
Koster	F1	71	Lemoenshoek	D2	60	Maclear	C3	66	Matatiele	D2	66
Kotzesrus	B3	62	Lentsweletau	H3	77	Madadeni	A3	75	Mateka	C1	66
Koukraal	F2	65	Lephepe	H2	77	Madiakgama	C1	71	Matjiesfontein	D1	60
Koup	E1	61	Letjiesbos	A5	64	Madibogo	D1	71	Matjiesrivier	F1	61
Koutjie	A5	60	Letlhakeng	F3	77	Madipelesa	C3	71	Matlabas	B3	79
Kraaifontein	B2	60	Letseng-La-Terae	D1	66	Mafeteng	B2	66	Matlala	D3	79
Kraaldorings	E1	61	Letsitele	B3	81	Mafikeng	E1	71	Matlameng	B5	73
Kraankuil	C2	65	Leydsdorp	B3	81	Mafube	D2	66	Matola	D1	75
Kransfontein	C4	73	Libertas	B4	73	Mafutseni	C2	75	Matroosberg	C1	60
Kranskop	G1	67	Libode	D4	66	Magaliesburg	A1	73	Matsaile	D2	66
Kriel	D1	73	Lichtenburg	E1	71	Magudu	C3	75	Matvhelo	C1	81
Kromdraai	D1	73	Lidgetton	F1	67	Magusheni	E3	67	Mavamba	C2	81
Kroonstad	A3	73	Limburg	D3	79	Mahalapye	A2	79	Mazenod	B1	66
Krugers	E2	65	Lime Acres	B4	70	Mahlabatini	B4	75	Mazeppa Bay	D5	66
Krugersdorp	B1	73	Linakeng	D1	66	Mahlangasi	C3	75	Mbabane	B1	75
Kruidfontein	F1	61	Lindeshof	C2	60	Mahwelereng	D3	79	Mbazwana	D3	75
Kruisfontein	D5	60	Lindley	B3	73	Maizefield	D2	73	McGregor	C2	60
Kruisrivier	F1	61	Lindleyspoort	A5	79	Makopong	D4	76	Mdantsane	G4	61
Ku-Mayima	C4	66	Llandudno	A2	60	Makwassie	E2	71	Meadows	F1	65
Kubung	C2	66	Lobamba	B2	75	Makwate	A2	79	Mekaling	B2	66
Kubutsa	B2	75	Lobatse	G4	77	Malaita	A4	81	Melkbosstrand	B2	60
Kuilsriver	B2	60	Loch Vaal	B2	73	Malealea	C2	66	Melmoth	B4	75
Kums	E3	69	Lochiel	B1	75	Maleoskop	D5	79	Meltonwold	A4	64
Kuruman	B3	70	Loerie	D5	60	Malgas	D3	60	Memel	D3	73
Kwa Dweshula	F3	67	Loeriesfontein	D3	63	Malmesbury	B1	60	Merindol	A1	73

Place	Grid	Page	Place	Grid	Page	Place	Grid	Page	Place	Grid	Page
Merweville	G5	63	Mortimer	E5	65	New Machavie	F2	71	Old Bunting	D4	66
Mesa	F1	71	Morupule	A1	79	Newcastle	D3	73	Old Morley	D4	66
Mesklip	B2	62	Morwamosu	D3	76	Newington	D4	81	Olifantshoek	A3	70
Messina	B1	81	Moshaneng	G4	77	Newsel-Umdloti	G2	67	Olyfberg	B3	81
Methalaneng	D1	66	Mosesh's Ford	C3	66	Ngabeni	E3	67	Omdraaisvlei	B2	64
Mevedja	D1	75	Mosita	D1	71	Ngobeni	B3	75	Onderstedorings	F2	63
Meyerton	B1	73	Mosomane	H3	77	Ngome	B3	75	Ons Hoop	B2	79
Mgwali	B5	66	Mosopa	G4	77	Ngqeleni	D4	66	Onseepkans	D4	68
Mhlambanyatsi	B2	75	Mossel Bay	A5	60	Ngqungu	D4	66	Ontmoeting	G2	69
Mhlosheni	B3	75	Mossiesdal	D5	79	Nhlangano	B2	75	Oorwinning	B1	81
Mhlume	C1	75	Motetema	A4	81	Nhlazatshe	B4	75	Oostermoed	A4	79
Mica	C3	81	Mothae	D1	66	Niekerkshoop	B1	64	Orania	C1	65
Middelburg	D1	73	Motokwe	D3	76	Nietverdiend	H4	77	Oranjefontein	B2	79
Middelburg	D4	65	Motshikiri	B5	79	Nieu-Bethesda	D4	65	Oranjemund	A4	68
Middelfontein	C4	79	Motsitseng	D1	66	Nieuwoudtville	D4	63	Oranjerivier	C1	65
Middelpos	E4	63	Mount Ayliff	E3	67	Nigel	C1	73	Oranjeville	B2	73
Middelwit	A4	79	Mount Fletcher	D3	66	Nigramoep	B1	62	Orkney	F2	71
Middleton	E4	61	Mount Frere	D3	66	Nkambak	B3	81	Osborn	B4	75
Midrand	B1	73	Mount Stewart	C4	60	Nkandla	B4	75	Osizweni	A3	75
Migdol	D2	71	Moyeni	C2	66	Nkau	C2	66	Otse	G4	77
Miller	C4	60	Mpaka Stn	C2	75	Nkomo	C2	81	Ottosdal	E2	71
Millvale	A5	79	Mpemvana	A3	75	Nkwalini	B5	75	Oudtshoorn	A5	60
Milnerton	B2	60	Mpendle	E1	67	Nobantu	D4	66	Oukraal	C3	60
Mirage	F2	71	Mpetu	C5	66	Nobokwe	C4	66	Ouplaas	D3	60
Misgund	B5	60	Mphaki	C2	66	Noenieput	E3	69	Overyssel	C2	79
Misty Mount	D4	66	Mpharane	B2	66	Nohana	C2	66	Oviston	E3	65
Mkambati	E4	67	Mpolweni	F1	67	Noll	A5	60	Owendale	B4	70
Mkuze	C3	75	Mpumalanga	F2	67	Nondweni	A4	75	Oxbow	C4	73
Mmamabula	A2	79	Mqanduli	D4	66	Nongoma	C3	75	Oyster Bay	D5	60
Mmathethe	G5	77	Mt Moorosi	C2	66	Noordhoek	A2	60	Paarl	B2	60
Moamba	D1	75	Mtonjaneni	B4	75	Noordkaap	B1	75	Pacaltsdorp	A5	60
Mochudi	H3	77	Mtubatuba	C4	75	Noordkuil	C5	62	Paddock	F3	67
Modderrivier	C5	71	Mtunzini	H1	67	Noordoewer	B4	68	Pafuri	D1	81
Moeng	B1	79	Mtwalume	F3	67	Normandien	D3	73	Pafuri Gate	C1	81
Moeswal	H3	69	Muden	F1	67	Northam	A4	79	Palala	C3	79
Mogalakwena	C3	79	Muizenberg	B2	60	Norvalspont	E3	65	Palapye	A1	79
Mogapi	B1	79	Munster	F3	67	Notintsila	D4	66	Paleisheuwel	C5	62
Mogapinyana	B1	79	Munyu	C4	66	Nottingham Road	E1	67	Palm Beach	F3	67
Mogwase	A5	79	Murchison	C3	81	Noupoort	D3	65	Palmerton	E4	67
Mohales Hoek	B2	66	Murraysburg	C4	65	Nqabara	D5	66	Palmietfontein	B2	66
Mokamole	C3	79	Mynfontein	C3	65	Nqabeni	E3	67	Pampierstad	C3	71
Mokhotlong	D1	66	Nababeep	B1	62	Nqamakwe	C5	66	Pampoenpoort	A3	64
Mokopung	C2	66	Nabies	E4	69	Nqutu	A4	75	Panbult	A2	75
Molepolole	G3	77	Naboomspruit	C4	79	Nsoko	C2	75	Pansdrif	B5	79
Moletsane	C1	66	Nakop	E3	69	Ntibane	D4	66	Papendorp	C4	62
Moloporivier	E5	77	Namaacha	C1	75	Ntseshe	C5	66	Papiesvlei	C3	60
Molteno	F4	65	Namakgale	C3	81	Ntshilini	E4	67	Papkuil	B4	70
Mont Pelaan	D3	73	Namies	D1	63	Ntywenke	D3	66	Park Rynie	F2	67
Montagu	D2	60	Napier	C3	60	Numbi Gate	C5	81	Parow	B2	60
Monte Christo	B2	79	Nariep	B3	62	Nutfield	C4	79	Parys	A2	73
Mooifontein	E1	71	Nature's Valley	B5	60	Nuwefontein	D3	68	Patensie	D5	60
Mooi River	E1	67	Ncanara	E5	61	Nuwerus	C3	62	Paternoster	A1	60
Mooketsi	B2	81	Ncora	C4	66	Nuy	C2	60	Paterson	E4	61
Moordkuil	C2	60	Ndumo	C2	75	Nylstroom	C4	79	Patlong	C2	66
Moorreesburg	B1	60	Ndundulu	B5	75	Nyokana	D5	66	Paul Kruger Gate	D4	81
Mopane	B1	81	Ndwedwe	G1	67	Oatlands	C4	60	Paul Roux	B4	73
Morgan's Bay	H4	61	Neilersdrif	F4	69	Obobogorap	E2	69	Paulpietersburg	B3	75
Morgenzon	D2	73	Nelspoort	B4	64	Odendaalsrus	F3	71	Pearly Beach	C3	60
Morija	B1	66	Nelspruit	C5	81	Ofcolaco	B3	81	Pearston	D5	65
Morokweng	B1	70	New Amalfi	D2	66	Ogies	C1	73	Peddie	F4	61
Morone	B4	81	New England	B3	66	Ohrigstad	B4	81	Peka	B5	73
Morristown	B4	66	New Hanover	F1	67	Okiep	B1	62	Pella	D5	68

Name	Grid	Pg	Name	Grid	Pg	Name	Grid	Pg	Name	Grid	Pg
Penge	B4	81	Pringle Bay	B3	60	Rietvlei	F1	67	Satco	D3	68
Pennington	F3	67	Priors	E2	65	Rita	D3	79	Sauer	B1	60
Perdekop	D2	73	Protem	D2	60	Ritchie	C5	71	Scarborough	A2	60
Petersburg	D5	65	Pudimoe	C2	71	Riversdale	E2	61	Scheepersnek	A3	75
Petrus Steyn	B3	73	Putsonderwater	G1	63	Riverside	E2	67	Schmidtsdrif	C4	71
Petrusburg	E1	65	Qabane	D2	66	Riverview	C4	75	Schoombee	E4	65
Petrusville	D2	65	Qacha's Nek	D2	66	Riviersonderend	C2	60	Schweizer-Reneke	D2	71
Phalaborwa	C3	81	Qamata	B4	66	Roamer's Rest	D2	66	Scottburgh	F2	67
Phamong	C2	66	Qiba	C4	66	Robert's Drift	C2	73	Sea Park	F3	67
Philadelphia	B2	60	Qobong	C2	66	Robertson	C2	60	Seaview	D5	60
Philippolis	D2	65	Qoboqobo	C5	66	Rode	D3	66	Sebapala	C2	66
Philippolis Road	E2	65	Qolora Mouth	C5	66	Rodenbeck	F1	65	Sebayeng	A3	81
Philipstown	C2	65	Qoqodala	B4	66	Roedtan	D4	79	Secunda	D1	73
Phitshane Molopo	G5	77	Qora Mouth	D5	66	Roma	C1	66	Sedgefield	A5	60
Phokwane	A4	81	Qudeni	B4	75	Rondevlei	A5	60	Seekoegat	A4	60
Phuthaditjhaba	C4	73	Queensburgh	G2	67	Roodebank	C2	73	Sefako	C4	73
Pienaarsrivier	C5	79	Queenstown	F4	65	Roodepoort	B1	73	Sefikeng	C1	66
Piet Plessis	C1	71	Quko	C5	66	Rooiberg	B4	79	Sehonghong	D1	66
Piet Retief	B2	75	Qumbu	D3	66	Rooibokkraal	A3	79	Sekhukhune	B4	81
Pieter Meintjies	D1	60	Radisele	A1	79	Rooibosbult	B3	79	Sekoma	E3	77
Pietermaritzburg	F1	67	Radium	C4	79	Rooigrond	E1	71	Selonsrivier	D5	79
Pietersburg	D3	79	Ralebona	C2	66	Rooikraal	D5	79	Sendelingsdrif	A4	68
Piggs Peak	B1	75	Raleqheka	C1	66	Rooipan	D1	65	Sendelingsfontein	E2	71
Piketberg	B1	60	Ramabanta	C1	66	Rooiwal	A2	73	Sending	D2	79
Pilane	H3	77	Ramatlabama	G5	77	Roosboom	D4	73	Senekal	A4	73
Pilgrim's Rest	C4	81	Ramotswa	H4	77	Roossenekal	B5	81	Sengwe	C1	81
Pinetown	F2	67	Ramsgate	F3	67	Rorke's Drift	A4	75	Senlac	E5	77
Pitsane	G5	77	Ranaka	G4	77	Rosebank	F2	67	Sentrum	A3	79
Pitseng	C1	66	Randalhurst	B4	75	Rosedene	A4	64	Seringkop	C5	79
Plaatbakkies	C2	62	Randburg	B1	73	Rosendal	B4	73	Serowe	A1	79
Plathuis	D2	60	Randfontein	B1	73	Rosetta	E1	67	Seshego	D3	79
Platrand	D2	73	Rankin's Pass	B4	79	Rosh Pinah	A3	68	Setlagole	D1	71
Plettenberg Bay	B5	60	Rashoop	B5	79	Rosmead	D4	65	Settlers	C4	79
Plooysburg	C5	71	Ratelfontein	C5	62	Rossouw	B3	66	Setuat	C2	71
Pniel	B2	60	Rawsonville	C2	60	Rostrataville	E2	71	Sevenoaks	F1	67
Pofadder	D1	63	Rayton	C5	79	Rothmere	D5	66	Severn	A1	70
Politsi	B3	81	Redcliffe	E1	67	Rouxpos	E1	61	Seweweekspoort	E1	61
Pomeroy	A4	75	Reddersburg	F1	65	Rouxville	F2	65	Seymour	F5	65
Pongola	C3	75	Redelinghuys	C5	62	Ruitersbos	F2	61	Sezela	F3	67
Ponta do Ouro	D2	75	Redoubt	E3	67	Rust	B1	60	Shaka's Rock	G1	67
Pools	B1	60	Reebokrand	D2	65	Rust de Winter	C5	79	Shakaskraal	G1	67
Port Alfred	F5	61	Reitz	B3	73	Rustenburg	A5	79	Shannon	F1	65
Port Beaufort	D3	60	Reitzburg	A2	73	Rustig	A3	73	Sheepmoor	A2	75
Port Edward	F3	67	Reivilo	C3	71	Rusverby	A5	79	Sheffield Beach	G1	67
Port Elizabeth	E5	61	Renosterkop	B5	64	Saaifontein	G4	63	Sheldon	E4	61
Port Grosvenor	E4	67	Renosterspruit	F2	71	Sabie	C5	81	Shelley Beach	F3	67
Port Nolloth	A1	62	Ressano Garcia	D5	81	Sada	F5	65	Sherborne	D3	65
Port Shepstone	F3	67	Restvale	B4	64	Sakrivier	E3	63	Sherwood Ranch	B1	79
Port St Johns	E4	67	Rex	A5	79	Salajwe	F2	77	Shoshong	H2	77
Porterville	B1	60	Richards Bay	H1	67	Salamanga	D2	75	Sicunusa	B2	75
Post Chalmers	E4	65	Richmond	C4	65	Saldanha	A1	60	Sidvokodvo	B2	75
Postmasburg	A4	70	Richmond	F2	67	Salem	F4	61	Sidwadweni	D4	66
Potchefstroom	F2	71	Riebeeckstad	F3	71	Salpeterpan	C2	71	Signalberg	C3	68
Potfontein	C2	65	Riebeek Kasteel	B1	60	Salt Lake	C1	65	Sigoga	D2	66
Potgietersrus	D3	79	Riebeek-Oos	E4	61	Salt Rock	G1	67	Sihoye	C1	75
Potsdam	G4	61	Riebeek-Wes	B1	60	Sand River Valley	D4	73	Sikwane	H4	77
Poupan	C2	65	Rietbron	B4	60	Sandberg	C5	62	Silent Valley	A4	79
Pr. Alfred Hamlet	C1	60	Rietfontein	E2	69	Sandton	B1	73	Silkaatskop	H4	77
Pretoria	C5	79	Rietkolk	D3	79	Sandvlakte	C5	60	Silutshana	A4	75
Prieska	A1	64	Rietkuil	C3	73	Sannaspos	F1	65	Silver Streams	B4	70
Prince Albert	F1	61	Rietpoel	C2	60	Sannieshof	E1	71	Simon's Town	B2	60
Prince Albert Road	E1	61	Rietpoort	B3	62	Sasolburg	B2	73	Sinksabrug	A5	60

Siphofaneni	C2	75	Steynsburg	E3	65	Thamaga	G4	77	Tylden	B5	66
Sir Lowry's Pass	B2	60	Steynsrus	A3	73	The Berg	C4	81	Tzaneen	B3	81
Sishen	A3	70	Steytlerville	C4	60	The Crags	B5	60	Ubombo	C3	75
Siteki	C2	75	Stilfontein	F2	71	The Downs	B3	81	Ugie	C3	66
Sithobela	C2	75	Still Bay East	E3	61	The Haven	D5	66	Uitenhage	D5	60
Sittingbourne	G4	61	Still Bay West	E3	61	The Heads	B5	60	Uitkyk	C1	62
Siyabuswa	D4	79	Stockpoort	A2	79	The Ranch	B5	75	Uitspankraal	D5	63
Skeerpoort	B5	79	Stoffberg	A5	81	Theron	F4	71	Ulco	C4	71
Skipskop	D3	60	Stofvlei	C2	62	Theunissen	F4	71	Ulundi	B4	75
Skuinsdrif	H5	77	Stompneusbaai	B5	62	Thohoyandou	B2	81	Umbogintwini	G2	67
Slurry	H5	77	Stoneyridge	D4	66	Thorndale	A2	81	Umbumbulu	F2	67
Smithfield	F2	65	Stormberg	F3	65	Thornville	F2	67	Umgababa	F2	67
Smitskraal	C5	60	Stormsrivier	C5	60	Three Sisters	B4	64	Umhlanga Rocks	G2	67
Sneeukraal	A4	64	Stormsvlei	D2	60	Tierfontein	E3	71	Umkomaas	F2	67
Sneezewood	E2	67	Straatsdrif	H5	77	Tierpoort	F1	65	Umlazi	G2	67
Sodium	B2	64	Strand	B2	60	Tina Bridge	D3	66	Umtata	D4	66
Soebatsfontein	B2	62	Strandfontein	C4	62	Tinmyne	C3	79	Umtentu	E4	67
Soekmekaar	B2	81	Struisbaai	C3	60	Tlali	C1	66	Umtentweni	F3	67
Sojwe	G2	77	Strydenburg	C2	65	Tlhakgameng	C1	71	uMzimkhulu	E2	67
Somerset East	E5	65	Strydpoort	E2	71	Tlokoeng	D1	66	uMzinto	F2	67
Somerset West	B2	60	Studtis	C4	60	Tolwe	C2	79	uMzumbe	F3	67
Somkele	C4	75	Stutterheim	B5	66	Tom Burke	B2	79	Underberg	E2	67
Sonop	B5	79	Summerstrand	E5	61	Tombo	E4	67	Uniondale	B5	60
Sonstraal	H2	69	Sun City/Lost City	A5	79	Tompi Seleka	D4	79	Upington	G4	69
Southbroom	F3	67	Sunland	E5	61	Tonash	C1	79	Usutu	C1	79
Southeyville	B4	66	Sutherland	F5	63	Tongaat	G1	67	Utrecht	A3	75
Southport	F3	67	Sutton	A2	70	Tontelbos	E3	63	Uvongo	F3	67
Southwell	F5	61	Suurbraak	D2	60	Tosca	C1	71	Vaalhoek	C4	81
Soutpan	B5	79	Swaershoek	E5	65	Tosing	C2	66	Vaalplaas	C5	79
Soutpan	E4	71	Swart Umfolozi	B3	75	Touwsriver	C1	60	Vaalwater	B3	79
Soweto	B1	73	Swartberg	E2	67	Trawal	C4	62	Val	C2	73
Spanwerk	A3	79	Swartkops	E5	61	Trichardt	D1	73	Valsrivier	B4	73
Spes Bona	F2	71	Swartmodder	F3	69	Trichardtsdal	B3	81	Van Reenen	D4	73
Spitskopvlei	D4	65	Swartplaas	F1	71	Triple Streams	D3	66	Van Rooyen	A4	75
Spoegrivier	B2	62	Swartputs	B4	70	Trompsburg	E2	65	Van Wyksdorp	E2	61
Spring Valley	F5	65	Swartruggens	A5	79	Tsatsu	F5	77	Van Wyksvlei	G2	63
Springbok	B1	62	Swartwater	C1	79	Tsazo	C4	66	Van Zylsrus	H2	69
Springfontein	E2	65	Swellendam	D2	60	Tsetsebjwe	C1	79	Vanalphensvlei	C3	79
Springs	C1	73	Swempoort	B3	66	Tsetseng	D2	76	Vanderbijlpark	B2	73
Spytfontein	C5	71	Swinburne	D4	73	Tshabong	H1	69	Vanderkloof	D2	65
St Faith's	F3	67	Syfergat	F4	65	Tshakhuma	B2	81	Vandyksdrif	D1	73
St Francis Bay	D5	60	Tabankulu	C1	75	Tshane	B3	76	Vanrhynsdorp	C4	62
St Helena Bay	C5	62	Tabankulu	E3	67	Tshaneni	C1	75	Vanstadensrus	B2	66
St Lucia	C4	75	Tafelberg	D4	65	Tshani	D4	66	Vant's Drift	A4	75
St Marks	B4	66	Tainton	H4	61	Tshidilamolomo	F5	77	Vegkop	B3	73
St Martin	D1	66	Takatokwane	E3	77	Tshipise	B1	81	Velddrif	A1	60
Staansaam	F2	69	Taleni	C5	66	Tshiturapadsi	C1	81	Ventersburg	F3	71
Stafford's Post	E3	67	Tarkastad	F4	65	Tsineng	A2	70	Ventersdorp	F1	71
Standerton	D2	73	Taung	D3	71	Tsitsa Bridge	D4	66	Venterskroon	A2	73
Stanford	C3	60	Temba	C5	79	Tsoelike	D2	66	Venterstad	E3	65
Stanger	G1	67	Tembisa	B1	73	Tsolo	D4	66	Vereeniging	B2	73
Steekdorings	C2	71	Terra Firma	D5	76	Tsomo	C5	66	Verena	D5	79
Steelpoort	B4	81	Teviot	E4	65	Tugela Ferry	A5	75	Vergeleë	E5	77
Steilloopbrug	C2	79	Tewane	A1	79	Tugela Mouth	G1	67	Verkeerdevlei	F4	71
Steilrand	B3	75	Teyateyaneng	C1	66	Tuinplaas	C4	79	Verkykerskop	D3	73
Steinkopf	B1	62	Teza	C4	75	Tunnel	C1	60	Vermaaklikheid	E3	61
Stella	D1	71	Thaba Bosiu	C1	66	Turton	F3	67	Vermaas	E1	71
Stellenbosch	B2	60	Thaba Chitja	C2	66	Twee Rivieren	F1	69	Verster	B4	64
Sterkaar	C3	65	Thaba 'Nchu	F1	65	Tweefontein	D5	63	Verulam	G2	67
Sterkspruit	B2	66	Thaba Tseka	D1	66	Tweeling	C3	73	Victoria West	B3	64
Sterkstroom	F4	65	Thabana Morena	B2	66	Tweespruit	B1	66	Viedgesville	D4	66
Sterling	G3	63	Thabazimbi	A4	79	Tyira	D3	66	Vier-en-Twintig Riv.	C3	79

Name	Grid	Page	Name	Grid	Page
Vierfontein	F2	71	Westonaria	B1	73
Viljoensdrif	B2	73	Weza	E3	67
Viljoenshof	C3	60	White River	C5	81
Viljoenskroon	F2	71	Whites	F3	71
Villa Nora	B2	79	Whitmore	C4	66
Villiers	C2	73	Whittlesea	F5	65
Villiersdorp	C2	60	Wiegenaarspoort	B5	64
Vineyard	F3	65	Wilderness	A5	60
Vioolsdrif	B4	68	Williston	F4	63
Virginia	F3	71	Willowmore	B4	60
Visrivier	E4	65	Willowvale	C5	66
Vivo	D2	79	Winburg	F4	71
Vleesbaai	F3	61	Wincanton	A3	70
Vleifontein	E1	61	Windmeul	B2	60
Vleiland	E1	61	Windsorton	C4	71
Volksrust	D3	73	Windsorton Road	D4	71
Volop	H4	69	Winkelpos	F3	71
Volstruisleegte	B4	60	Winterton	D5	73
Voortrekkerspos	A3	79	Winterveld	B5	79
Vorstershoop	D5	76	Witbank	D1	73
Vosburg	B2	64	Witdraai	F2	69
Vrede	C3	73	Witkop	F3	65
Vredefort	A2	73	Witmos	E5	65
Vredenburg	A1	60	Witnek	D5	79
Vredendal	C4	62	Witpoort	E2	71
Vredesdorp	E2	69	Witput	C1	65
Vroeggedeel	H3	69	Witpütz	A3	68
Vrouenspan	F3	69	Witsand	D3	60
Vryburg	C2	71	Wittedrif	B5	60
Vryheid	A3	75	Witteklip	D5	60
Waenhuiskrans	D3	60	Witwater	C2	62
Wakkerstroom	A3	75	Wolmaransstad	E2	71
Walkerville	B1	73	Wolplaas	D3	68
Wallekraal	B2	62	Wolseley	B1	60
Wanda	C1	65	Wolvepoort	F2	65
Waqu	B5	66	Wolwefontein	D4	60
Warburton	A1	75	Wolwehoek	B2	73
Warden	C3	73	Wolwespruit	D4	71
Warm Baths	C4	79	Wonderfontein	A5	81
Warmbad	D4	68	Wonderkop	A3	73
Warmwaterberg	D2	60	Wondermere	H5	77
Warrenton	D3	71	Woodlands	C5	60
Wasbank	A4	75	Wooldridge	G4	61
Waterford	D4	60	Worcester	C2	60
Waterkloof	E2	65	Woudkop	C2	79
Waterpoort	A2	81	Wuppertal	D5	63
Waterval-Boven	B5	81	Wyford	D4	73
Wavecrest	C5	66	Xolobe	C5	66
Waverley	B1	75	Yzerfontein	A1	60
Wegdraai	H4	69	Zaaimansdal	B5	60
Welgeleë	F4	71	Zastron	B2	66
Welkom	F3	71	Zebediela	D3	79
Wellington	B2	60	Zeerust	H5	77
Welverdiend	A1	73	Zitundo	D2	75
Wepener	B1	66	Zoar	E1	61
Werda	D4	76	Zunckels	D5	73
Wesley	G4	61	Zwartkop	F2	63
Wesselsbron	F3	71	Zwarts	E1	61
Wesselsvlei	B2	70	Zwelitsha	G4	61
Westerberg	A1	64	Zwingli	H4	77
Westleigh	A3	73			
Westminster	B1	66			